A SHEPHERD'S JOURNEY

AN EXPLORATION OF I PETER 5:1-4
ILLUSTRATING MORAL PRINCIPLES AND MISSIONAL PURPOSE

STEVE CRAWFORD

WestBow
P R E S S
A DIVISION OF THOMAS NELSON

WestBow Press books may be ordered through booksellers or by contacting:

WestBow Press
A Division of Thomas Nelson
1663 Liberty Drive
Bloomington, IN 47403
www.westbowpress.com
1-(866) 928-1240

ISBN: 978-1-4497-7572-8 (e)
ISBN: 978-1-4497-7571-1 (sc)
ISBN: 978-1-4497-7573-5 (hc)

Library of Congress Control Number: 2012921305

Printed in the United States of America

WestBow Press rev. date: 12/11/2012

A SHEPHERD'S JOURNEY

DEDICATION

Dedicated to the ever-present, great shepherd Jesus Christ and all that are called into His service. The author expresses special appreciation for godly educators at the graduate seminary. Two of the best friends, mentors, and spiritual guides a person could know: Bob and David. Most importantly to my loving, faithful, and encouraging wife Tammy, whose dedication and talents made this a reality; to my beloved son and best buddy Jason, who will always have his dad's heart; to my dear family and church who have partnered with me throughout the years. All of whom have played a priceless role in a shepherd's journey.

CONTENTS

INTRODUCTION

AS A YOUNG MINISTER OUT of Bible college, I was introduced to a colorful, dramatic literary work written by Harold Bell Wright. His *Shepherd of the Hills* was set in the beautiful Ozark Mountains. Wright describes a pastor who left a world of cities, modern conveniences, and cutting-edge technology, along with a successful lifestyle, only to step into a backward, simplified world of hill folk. He serves a well-known local family, tending their sheep in Mutton Hollow. The pastor encounters these backwoodsy characters which the family doesn't withhold their forthright opinions, and discover a real beauty and peacefulness in their simple way of life. A series of gripping situations and thrilling incidents leads to a connection with the locals, establishing successful relationships.

The shepherd of this story serves as a reminder not to forget the simple concepts that reflect the essence of spiritual leadership on a primal level. It may take courage for today's spiritual leaders to step back and revisit the basic principles that led them into their service. One will possibly find a fresh challenge to boil things down to a simple yet effective service among a deluge of the many modern distractions, advances, methods, and changing cultures today.

Shepherding the flock in the postmodern era proves to be a viable and indispensably gifted role. The leader is given for the church's survival and successful mission. Postmodern society's perception of a pastor conveys the idea of a professional vocation, and rightly so. The shepherd strives to remain current concerning issues of government regulations regarding pastor, church, and law relationships, spanning fiscal health management to safety in the sanctuary and the newest cultural transformations.

The congregational leader learns to integrate superlative executive management and coaching skills in combination with technological-driven multimedia sources ranging from simple PowerPoint presentations to podcasts to animated productions. He or she networks with cohorts and fosters relationships that enable success in his or her personal and professional arena. The high-tech-savvy modern shepherd continues to set pace with the latest trends of communication skills and effectively update methods to present the relevant gospel of Christ to a postmodern, pluralistic, changing world.

The image of shepherding the flock is applied to congregational leadership. The biblical metaphor of a shepherd is an appropriate description of a pastor. When a postmodern pastor rediscovers the basic principles entrusted to shepherd God's people, renewed primal concepts begin to surface. The relevant insights bridge the gap from a biblical view of shepherding the flock to the modern servant leader discovering practical applications for initiating fresh awareness and encouragement to the task.

Pastoral leaders hold sacred trust, influencing and equipping the church for an effective ministry enabled by the Holy Spirit. A study of 1 Peter 5:1–4 reflects the implications of the spiritual formation, practice, leadership, role, and reward of the pastor with insightful moral, practical, and missional applications. The emphasis of this passage is asserted in verse 2: "Be shepherds of God's flock that is under your care."[1] Though the lead chair of the church is prominent in this script, there are timeless

---

1   All scripture is quoted from New International Version unless noted otherwise.

principles that can be applied to all churchmen and laity engaged in ministry.

Peter was concerned that leadership should be at its best. The apostle wrote this unique message to the leaders of the church to encourage them to do their work faithfully: "Peter's message to his readers is that their 'home', that is their identity is found in the 'family of God' which is the fellowship of God's people, a 'spiritual house'. Paradoxically, these 'resident aliens' are also God's 'chosen people'. Their identity represents an effort to equip the church for the fulfillment of its mission."[2] The flock's dependency to express their faith in Christ for their collective welfare became paramount, which also developed interdependency with strong communal ties toward one another.

The pastor's task in relation to the flock was joined with many personal hardships and occasionally exposed the spiritual leaders to public endangerment. Times of persecution demand that God's people have sufficient spiritual leadership. When the fiery trial would come, the believers in the assemblies would look to their elders for encouragement and direction. The shepherd's courage and faithfulness assured the Christian community that their best interests were paramount and not founded in the pastor's own vain, selfish desires.

Tough times expose the exact character of servant leadership, setting apart the true and faithful from the phony and self-serving. Leaders who run away in times of trouble only prove they are hirelings and not true shepherds. The servant leaders who remain steadfast through difficult circumstances do so knowing that their calling is an election sure. The lead chair is more than a vocation; it presupposes a purpose-driven life of service.

Peter begins his identification with the elders' call to service that sparks an encouraging charge to be diligent in their duties to the flock.

---

2   Andreas J. Köstenberger and Peter T. O'Brien, *Salvation to the Ends of the Earth* (Downers Grove, Ill.: InterVarsity Press, 2006), 238.

His address to the leaders of the church resounds with encouragement, faith, and hope, yet fosters them to follow Christ's example of suffering and enduring hardships innocently, honorably, and nobly. The shepherds and their flocks were highly tempted to return to the world from which they came, renouncing their faith so as to protect their lives and property. Peter warns the shepherds to beware of the temptations that would prohibit them from their primary purpose of feeding the flock, knowing a far greater reward awaits the faithful shepherd.

Historical/Cultural Background

INVESTIGATION OF THE HISTORICAL SETTING of 1 Peter 5:1–4 will assist our exploration of the implications found in this passage. The authenticity of the apostle Peter's authorship of the manuscript bearing his name has been questioned. However, many commentators have argued in favor of his authorship, stating that early evidence supports the view that Peter was in fact the letter's author, and that it fits well within Peter's lifetime. The authorship of 1 Peter is testified by Peter himself, writing the letter with the assistance of Silas as his scribe around 60–63 A.D.

Simon Peter is one of the best-known individuals of the early church. He grew up in Bethsaida along the coast of Galilee where he and his brother Andrew were vocational fishermen. Andrew introduced Simon to Jesus, and the Lord renamed him Petros or "Rock." While living in Capernaum, Jesus personally called Peter to the ministry, and he was appointed one of the original twelve apostles. He became part of Christ's inner circle and appeared to be the voice for the twelve.

Peter was endowed with strength, courage, and seemingly overconfidence, only to deny that he knew Christ when intimidated by a servant girl during the final hours of Jesus' life. His faith was restored and strengthened after the resurrection of Christ by numerous appearances of the risen Savior.

On the day of Pentecost, Peter stood boldly and preached the first-recorded Christian message, with three thousand people receiving salvation. He administered bold leadership in the church by working miracles in Jesus' name (Acts 3:11–16), with his strong defense of the faith (Acts 4:8–12), and having experienced extreme maltreatment and suffering (Acts 5:17–18). While his primary ministry was to the Jews, he assisted in opening the church to the Gentiles.

"The tradition of Peter's martyrdom in Rome is virtually unanimous. I Clement, by the late first century, accepted the letter's authenticity, and excavations indicate a second-century memorial in Rome to Peter's martyrdom."[3] He probably penned the letter from Rome prior to his death under Nero.

The first-century church was split by two cultures that would draw the Jewish and Gentile people to become one in Christ. The first believers, primarily Jewish, grew after the resurrection of Christ as a faction of Judaism. The Messianic Jewish community was caught off-guard by the fact that God would allow the pagan outsiders to become a part of the chosen people by their faith in Christ just as He had received them.

The church grew, changing the dynamics of its constituents where, in many places, Gentiles predominated. Exploration of the new faith's relationship to Greek philosophies and ways surfaced. The reality of Christ became superior to the cosmology of the heathen and to the revealed

3   C. S. Keener, *First Peter* (electronic ed.). (Downers Grove, Ill.: InterVarsity Press, 1993), 705.

shadow truths of the Jews. Gentile and Jewish Christians began to shake off old identities, finding a new common bond in Christ alone, but not without struggling through their cultural and traditional differences. The affirmation of the superiority of Christ as the central focus of faith became the heartbeat of the new Christian society.

Peter addresses this letter to "strangers" scattered throughout the Roman provinces of Asia Minor south of the Black Sea (modern Turkey). He responded to the growing opposition against Christianity and the lack of official governmental support. The readers were mostly Gentile Christians who had previously become attached to Judaism through local synagogues as God-fearers. It is likely that the road to Christianity for these Gentile pagans may have included a stop at the local synagogue where they were instructed in the Torah and the Jewish lifestyle. However, it is also likely that the letter was sent to mixed communities composed of Greek Christians and dispersed Hebrew Christians living in major Gentile cities.

HOMELESS SITUATION

THE SOCIETY OF STRANGERS WAS suddenly homeless, disconnected, discredited, discouraged, persecuted, and marginalized for their faith in Christ. Some experienced for the first time what it was like to be foreigners and exiles, losing what world they had in exchange for an eternal home elsewhere. As the old spiritual song resounds, "This world is not my home, I'm just passing through." They would be encouraged not to mourn what they might lose but rejoice in the glory to come.

Peter gave life instructions for the Christian pilgrims along their journey as opposed to the life of the world they traveled through. He encouraged them to be amenable to God and not disobedient (1:14, 22). To endeavor to be holy as opposed to living the unholy life of the world (1:15). To be as servants in this world not self-centered people (2:16; 4:11); to trust God through prayer as opposed to refusing God (3:7; 4:7); to live an open translucent existence rather than living deviously (2:16; 3:16); to do what is right and good as opposed to what is wide of the mark (2:15; 3:16–17); to be temperate and respectful rather than living ruthlessly or disrespectfully (3:15).

He also advices them to love one another genuinely and give no place for hatred (1:22; 4:8); to exercise self-discipline instead of living excessively and uncontrollably (1:13; 4:7; 5:8); to live meekly and not pompously or egotistically (5:6); to refuse evil and oppose acceptance of wickedness (2:11); to agree to human rule instead of rejecting authority

5

(2:13, 17); to be in charge of one's own corrupt desires instead of allowing them complete freedom (2:1, 11). He exhorted them to do the Lord's will instead of rejecting and disobeying it (4:2); to share with others liberally rather than squirreling away belongings (4:9); to use charity and talents for others as opposed to refusing to do so (4:10–11). This new way of life set the Christian society apart in a multicultural pluralistic pagan world.

These believers are called aliens and strangers who reside as ones without rights, referring to the state or fate of a person dwelling abroad who has no rights in the country in which he or she resides. John Elliott who is Professor Emeritus of New Testament at the University of San Francisco refers to the displaced believers by stating: "This would be true of those who were required to reside permanently away from their homeland without the full protection and rights they once enjoyed, as in the case of Abraham among the Hittites, Moses in Midian and the Israelites in Egypt."[4] This status for God's faithful people was normal in the history of Israel, even if it was the result of God's hand.

In the Roman Empire these terms were used for the group of resident aliens below citizen status and above that of slaves and foreigners. According to Scot McKnight, Elliott says:

> Legally, such aliens were restricted in regard to whom they could marry, the holding of land and succession of property, voting, and participation in certain associations and were subjected to higher taxes and severer forms of civil punishment. Set apart from their host society by their lack of local roots, their ethnic origin, language, culture, and political or religious loyalties, such strangers were commonly viewed as threats to established order and native well-being. Constant exposure to local fear and suspicion, ignorant

---

4   John H. Elliott, *A Home for the Homeless* (Eugene, Ore.: Wipf and Stock Publishers, 2005), 26.

slander, discrimination and manipulation was the regular lot of these social outsiders.[5]

Their homeless situation would have also been a picture of these believers' spiritual status. The believers were castaways because of their commitment to Jesus, living a separate holy life. They were viewed with suspicion not only socially but religiously, as their God were unlike the idols of the day.

The Romans often held the same opinion of Christians as they did Jews by classifying them as a sect not socially recognized by the state. They stereotyped Christians as atheists because of their refusal to worship idols, said they were cannibalistic because they ate the body and drinking the blood of Christ, and thought them to be incestuous for possessing a love for the brethren which they expressed using phrases like, "I love you, brother or sister."

The traditional orthodox Jewish communities having a certain disdain among the Roman citizenry had grown in popularity and numbers and were no longer a primary object of blatant persecution. However, Christians who were associated with Judaism became new political scapegoats and incurred great suffering. Peter recognized the persecutions with its struggles as spiritual warfare against evil forces and fleshly desires that war against the soul (1 Peter 2:11).

---

5   Scot McKnight, *I Peter* (Grand Rapids, Mich.: Zondervan, 1984), 25.

HABITAT JESUS

THE SPIRIT LED THE JUDEO-CHRISTIANS out of homelessness to a new habitat; a household of faith that is the family of God was established. They would obtain acceptance and sanctuary among themselves, discovering their new life in Christ Jesus. Peter points out that the believers, composed of both believing Jews and Gentiles, are the people of God, the true spiritual house of Israel which is one people. "Peter describes the church with terms that have been used in defining Israel. They are the 'elect' and 'scattered' ones (1:1) and a 'holy priesthood' (2:5). Most prominent here is 2:9–10: 'You are a chosen people, a royal priesthood, a holy nation, belonging to God. ... Once you were not a people but now you are the people of God; once you had not received mercy, but now you have received mercy.'"[6]

This is the language of fulfillment regarding the displaced Gentile converts who now found themselves merging with Jewish believers while entering into a greater household of faith.

> Peter uses a number of images, mostly drawn from the OT, to depict and illume the situation and responsibilities of his readers. The metaphor that controls these images is Israel, the people of God. This metaphor expresses itself in four aspects: (1) that the believers as the spiritual Israel do not belong to this world, (2) that they do belong in

---

6   McKnight, 24.

God's house (Israel) by identification with Jesus Christ, (3) that God has graciously brought them into that state of belonging and (4) that such a situation results in a kind of warfare.[7]

Peter's purpose for the letter was one of joyful hope, providing believers with a divine and eternal outlook on their earthly lives. He desired to provide practical guidance to those who were beginning to experience a fiery trial of suffering as Christians in a heathen society. "Christians are viewed as 'disgraced yet graced' and reminded of the dignity and honor they already enjoy as members of God's household. They are also enjoined to solidarity with their shamed but divinely honored Lord Jesus Christ."[8] These believers experienced daily hardships and were feed a diet of humble pie, even though they were right and faithful in their lifestyle, while the pagan Romans and other outside influences brought them grave harassment.

Peter's concern was that believers not provoke governmental structures unnecessarily, yet following Christ's example in suffering blamelessly. "For the harassed Christian movement in Asia Minor to survive and grow, isolated pockets of believers throughout the provinces required a sense of the ties which bound them in a common cause. If Christians were to resist external pressures and be mutually supportive, a high degree of group consciousness was essential."[9] A community of faith banding together can withstand and overcome social pressures that otherwise could lead to its deterioration or demise.

It becomes important for the people of God to find those who have fallen through the social cracks and then to minister God's acceptance to

7   L. Ryken, J. Wilhoit, T. Longman, C. Duriez, D. Penney, and D. G. Reid. *Dictionary of Biblical Imagery, Letter of First Peter* (electronic ed.). (Downers Grove, Ill.: InterVarsity Press, 2000), 637.

8   Köstenberger and O'Brien, 238. Author attributes J. H. Elliott (1995) for "Disgraced Yet Graced. The Gospel According to I Peter in the Key of Honor and Shame", *BTB* 25, 166-178.

9   Elliott, 133.

them, signifying that the Lord's true family transcends and negates the social boundaries society constructs. The people of God are indicative of the family where all can be accepted and discover a fresh way of existence with a new found habitat in Jesus. The habitation provides a situation that fosters love, acceptance, and forgiveness which is the fertile soil of the Christian communities.

Out of the rubble of persecution, a new socioeconomic existence occurs. These resident aliens have a "new home and social family to which the Christians belong here and now. This home and communal experience of salvation which it signifies are not 'beyond time and history,' but are already at hand in the community which is 'in Christ' (3:16; 5:10, 14)."[10] Howard Marshall suggests the household of faith is one where each member is interdependent.

> Peter's comments on leadership in the church raises questions about his readers' relationships to their church leaders and to one another. And Peter does have something to say to the younger members of the congregation and then to everybody. His pattern of teaching again resembles that of a Household Code, a set of instructions for the different member of a family, including its servants, that outlines their duties toward one another (as in 2:11–3:12). The 'household' pattern is used ecclesiastically here as the basis for harmony within the whole church.[11]

The household represents an example of a voluntarily cooperative fellowship with strong interrelations that achieve the community's common goals, which are relevant for unity and service today. "The Bible provides a rich kaleidoscope of imagery about the church composed of around one hundred metaphors and statements. The thread on which all other jewels are hung is the idea of the church as an *ekkl sia* ("assembly,"

---

10   Elliott, 130.
11   I. Howard Marshall, *The IVP New International Commentary Series: I Peter* (Downers Grove, Ill: InterVarsity Press, 1991), 159.

"gathering")."[12] The common use is applied to the calling out of citizens for civic meetings or the call for soldiers to come together for battle.

"A key New Testament term for church is *ekkl sia*, derived: *ek* is 'out' and *kaleo* is 'to call.' The LXX used to translate Hebrew *kahal* (also *qahal*), the community of Israel. In Greek setting it is used for assembly of the city-state (hence 'Assembly of God'). *Ekklesia* can mean the church universal, the local church, and the church in a particular city or region."[13] The church is an amalgamation of people worldwide believing and practicing a faith in the lordship of Jesus Christ who share His mission of compassion, discipleship, evangelism, and worship.

Dr. Edgar R. Lee defines the church as "the entire body of persons through all ages who have been regenerated, united, and energized by the Holy Spirit under the Lordship of Jesus Christ."[14] "For by one Spirit we were all baptized into one body ... and we were all made to drink of one Spirit" (1 Corinthians 12:13). The church is a spiritual living organism created by the living God, existing and thriving by the enablement of the Holy Spirit. All constituents of the church have entered the same way by a phenomenal and instantaneous act of God possessing equal value and status.

"Karl Barth noted that one of the several ways in which the church witnesses to Jesus Christ is simply by its existence."[15] The church exists because of the creative act of Jesus Christ who after His ascension gave the church its birth by sending the Holy Spirit on the Day of Pentecost (Acts 2:4). The church is referred to a people called out and summoned together as citizens of God's kingdom. Ephesians 2:19 says "You are no

---

12 L. Ryken, J. Wilhoit, T. Longman, C. Duriez, D. Penney, and D. G. Reid, *Dictionary of Biblical Imagery* (electronic ed.). (Downers Grove, Ill.: InterVarsity Press, 2000), 147.

13 Edgar R. Lee, STD, "Systematic Theology II." (Class notes for Unit 4 Ecclesiology at Assemblies of God Theological Seminary, Springfield, Mo., July 3, 2008).

14 Ibid.

15 Millard J. Erickson, *Christian Theology,* 2nd ed. (Grand Rapids, Mich.: Baker Books, 1998), 1036.

longer foreigners and aliens, but fellow citizen with God's people and members of God's household."

"When we encounter the church, we move into spiritual territory that occupies earthly terrain. We enter the living God in the midst of our humanity. We encounter the Spirit of God dwelling in the midst of a people who are created and formed into a unique community."[16] The convert begins participating with a collective dimension of believers who are practitioners of the Christ way of life. The people of God or the church is defined as a local community of faith and is given a broader designation including all believers spanning time and distance.

The local sense of the church is evident given that Paul addressed specific gathering places of believers. The apostle, for example, refers to "the church of God in Corinth" (1 Corinthians 1:2; 2 Corinthians 1:1), "the churches in Galatia" (Galatians 1:2), and to individuals like Priscilla and Aquila who allowed the church to meet in their homes. A proper explanation for the church is "a community of people who stand firm in the truth over time against raging currents of opposition and who present living proof of a loving God to a watching world."[17]

The church finds its expression in local assemblies; however it is universal in nature, defining the body of Christ as a whole. In the broader sense the church is one significant body throughout the world that simultaneously includes every local community. The theologian Karl Schmidt asserts, "We have pointed out that the sum of the individual congregations does not produce the total community or the church. Each community, however small, represents the total community, the church."[18]

---

16   Craig Van Gelder, *The Essence of the Church* (Grand Rapids, Mich.: Baker Books, 2007), 14.
17   Robert Lewis, *The Church of Irresistible Influence*. (Grand Rapids, Mich.: Zondervan, 2001), 41.
18   Erickson, 1043.

The standard process to become a part of the church was to have faith in Christ for salvation. This is confirmed in Acts 2:47: "And the Lord added to their number daily those who were being saved." The emphasis is placed on "the importance of every believer's becoming an integral part of a group of believers, and making a firm commitment to it. Christianity is a corporate matter, and the Christian life can be fully realized only in relationship to others."[19]

In the view of visible local churches and the acknowledgement of the universality of the church, how do we determine the marks of a real church? Unity and holiness mark the church affected by the Holy Spirit under Christ's rule and are to be guarded by all means (Ephesians 4:3). It was Martin Luther who set a priority on the distinction of who represents the visible and invisible church. "He suggested that the true church consists only of the justified, those savingly related to God."[20] The invisible church is the body of true believers united cross-culturally by faith and transcending denominational and geographical barriers.

The visible church is a composite of local congregates who make outward professions of the lordship of Christ. Christians assemble to hear the Word, celebrating the sacraments and baptism known as ordinances of the church. "A church is no longer a true church when it abandons the functions of a church. Things such as preaching and observing the Lord's Supper and baptism are not simply optional functions in a church. They are marks of the true church."[21] Christians must continually observe and never compromised or discard these scriptural mandates for any reason or cause.

Water baptism is a token of salvation that is an outward symbolic act indicating the spiritual change that has occurred in the believer, implying newness of life in Christ (Romans 6:4). "Baptism means identifying with

---

19   Ibid.,, 1058.
20   Ibid., 1054.
21   Elmer L. Towns and Ed Stetzer, *Perimeters of Light Biblical Boundaries for the Emerging Church* (Chicago, Ill.: Moody Publishers, 2004), 70–71.

Christ in His death and burial in order that we may live in union with his resurrected life."[22] The method of baptism is full immersion, and the formula is "in the name of the Father, Son, and Holy Spirit."

The Lord's Supper implicates the real presence of Christ (1 Corinthians 11:23–26). "The Lord's Supper as an ordinance is a unique opportunity to meet with Him. The Lord's Supper proclaims his (1) death, and (2) return. His presence by His Spirit is to be uniquely anticipated and celebrated."[23] The Lord's Supper involves a fellowship with Christ participating in His sacrificial benefits and fellowshipping with other believers. The results of communion reaffirm faith in Christ, assuring one's commitment to explicitly follow His will, resisting sin and identifying with the mission of God.

As a divinely established institution, the church's role is the continuation of the Lord's presence and ministry on Earth. The heart of the church's ministry is the gospel message it proclaims. Jesus charged His followers to continue delivering the good news that He initiated through His ministry of teaching and preaching. "The Spirit-led, missional church participates in God's mission in the world. In doing so, it becomes a *sign* that God's redemption is now present in the world, a *foretaste* of what that redemption is like, and an *instrument* to carry that message into every local context and to the ends of the earth."[24]

The good news is "a message that does not become obsolete, it is the church's sacred trust today. In an age in which most ideas and systems of thought, as well as techniques and commodities, are of a throwaway variety, the church has an infallible and enduring resource—a message that is the only means of salvation."[25] When the church remains focused

---

22   *The Full Life Study Bible, King James Version* (Zondervan, 1998), 1737.

23   Lee, July 3, 2008.

24   Craig Van Gelder, *The Ministry of the Missional Church* (Grand Rapids, Mich.: BakerBooks, 2007), 19.

25   Erickson, 1074.

on its primary role proclaiming the gospel message, a balance within its missions exist.

Peter's "appeal is made to sacred Scripture, common religious traditions, established rites and practices, divine norms, sanctions, and distinctive features of Christian faith and fraternity in order to motivate Christian segregation from the 'sinners' and solidarity among the faithful."[26] His perspective is that Christians should live for the salvation that is to come. This is indicative of the social context of the family of God. The unification of this new social network after its members were rejected by an unjust, cruel world now breeds a sense of belonging, hope, and purpose into a lifestyle that is conducive to the believers' habitation in Jesus. It is God who judges justly and will reward those who faithfully endure suffering for His sake. Peter assures believers that for righteous suffering they will obtain God's favor and reward.

---

26 Elliott, 107.

Analysis and Explanation of 1 Peter 5:1–4

To the elders among you, I appeal as a fellow elder, a witness of Christ's sufferings and one who also will share in the glory to be revealed: Be shepherds of God's flock that is under your care, serving as overseers—not because you must, but because you are willing, as God wants you to be; not greedy for money, but eager to serve; not lording it over those entrusted to you, but being examples to the flock. And when the Chief Shepherd appears, you will receive the crown of glory that will never fade away.

LITERARY CONTEXT

THE LITERARY CONTEXT OF 1 Peter 5:1–4 is linked to the previous passages in 4:12–19. Here Peter comforted those who were suffering for being Christians and encouraged them to look for Christ's return as the end was near. "The original readers of 1 Peter were suffering abuse for their faith, and needed to 'know how things really are'. Their experience is placed within the framework of the real world constituted by God the creator who has acted in Christ, who is presently at work within them, and who takes responsibility to bring the world to a worthy conclusion."[27] The reality of the struggle in the here and now merges with the glorious consummation of a faithful life.

Peter urged the flock to love one another deeply and was not surprised at the painful trial they were incurring "Above all, love each other deeply, because love covers over a multitude of sins" (1 Peter 4:8). "The Christians Peter was writing to may have been suffering grief from various trials. Whatever the case, he reassures them that God has a special grace to minister to each trial with its attendant grief. That grace, however, flows through people to people."[28] God's grace is truly more than sufficient as it descends upon faithful Christians who accept their struggles and

---

27   M. Eugene Boring, *Abingdon New Testament Commentaries: 1 Peter* (Nashville, Tenn.: Abingdon Press, 1999), 184. Boring acknowledges Elliott's contribution with the phrase "know how things really are," Elliott 1981, 19–20.

28   David Lim, *Spiritual Gifts: A Fresh Look* (Springfield, Mo.: Gospel Publishing House, 2003), 210.

weaknesses for the gospel's sake. The greater the believers' trials or weaknesses, the more grace God will grant them to attain His will. His great grace is sufficient enough to live out our daily lives as we labor and endure sufferings for Him (2 Corinthians 12:9).

Peter explains that judgment should start with the house of God (1 Peter 4:17), as it will purify the church from the unfaithful and allow believers to remain faithful through it all. "Some believers live with the daily threat of persecution for their faith. To them, 1Peter is a precious letter of pastoral encouragement from the heart of an apostle, helping them understand their calling as followers of Christ. If suffering for Christ should be the believer's experience, Peter reframes it as a reason not for bitterness or despair but for joy (4:13)."[29] Instead of being disheartened due to their helplessness, displacement and mistreatment from the world, the believers received encouragement and strength in their faith looking toward the future."

Regarding the church, Lauri Thurén a scholar says, "If the addresses have to suffer, they should do so as Christians and not as criminals. In so doing they take part in the sufferings of Christ and consequently in his glory. This should give them reason to rejoice and praise God, of which 1:3–12 speak as a fact. The joy in turn leads to endurance in the sufferings."[30]

The empowered community of faith is now postured to minister to an offensive world without receiving a defensive and defeated mentality.

> The good news of the Kingdom is that the whole of Christ's work is a work of liberation from the rule of sin, Satan, and death. Hence, the church must reflect liberation from the influence of the "dominion of darkness." The church in our day must be called back to "true spiritual violence, based on earnest faith: faith in the possibility of a miracle, in the Lordship of Jesus Christ, and in the coming of the

---

29 Karen H. Jobes, *I Peter* (Grand Rapids, Mich.: Baker Academic, 2005), 287.
30 Lauri Thurén, "Argument and Theology in I Peter: The Origins of Christian Paraenesis," *Journal for the Study of the New Testament* 114, (1995), 178–181.

Kingdom through God's action." This means "faith in all of the promises" implied and guaranteed by the resurrection. As the Body of Christ, we are to continue the mission of the Incarnate One in the world today and that includes an ongoing offensive against the fallen principalities and powers, a vigorous, active use of power in the search for greater justice in society.[31]

The passage (5:1–4) tells the leadership of the church what is required to guarantee the survival of the flock in difficult times of persecution. "Peter assumes that there will be leaders in the church. He does not discuss how they are appointed or what their duties are. He is concerned, as so often in biblical discussions of leadership, with how they do their appointed duties. It is the style of the leadership that matters. The main point is the way in which leadership is exercised."[32] Character and integrity are two fundamental components necessary to exercise effective leadership that unleash perimeters of influence into multifaceted spheres adding to one's credibility.

Elders should willingly shepherd the people under their care, not for personal gain but as an example of Christ's likeness. "Peter underscores the importance of responsible church structure for seeing the Christian community safely through the fiery ordeal of testing."[33] Shepherds should faithfully care for the flock knowing the chief shepherd will come with His rewards.

Following this pastoral exhortation, Peter speaks of the responsibilities those who are being led have (5:5–11). A walk of humility is required, displaying the absence of pride in oneself and consciousness of one's weakness that allow us to invoke our dependence upon Christ and interdependence with one another. Peter encourages us to bind the cloth

---

31   Arthur F. Glasser, *Announcing the Kingdom.* (Grand Rapids, Mich.: Baker Academic, 2007), 340 –341.
32   Marshall, 159.
33   Jobes, 299.

of humility toward others receiving God's grace and help. Here Peter may have had in mind Jesus taking up the towel to wash his, Peter's, feet.

To receive their future reward (5:4) and heavenly home, the believers find themselves dependent upon one another maintaining their fellowship in the Lord here and now. Their maintenance should come in the form of submission to one another. "Peter was aware of differences between elders and the 'younger ones' and urged them to submit as a principle consistent with true spiritual leadership.... When both elders and laity are out to serve, the elders are no more authoritarian than the laity is rebellious."[34]

The believers were to be humble in all their relationships, as God opposes the proud but cares for His own. Believers were also to band together and resist the Devil, standing firm in the faith. Having addressed the proper response of the Christians in Asia Minor to both the cultural conflict and suffering under persecution they faced, Peter now turns his attention to matters regarding the church realizing that pressure on a community and leadership can often cause deterioration in that community.

He shows the elders how to conduct their lives when facing adversity and fierce trials. Postmodern shepherds can expect challenges in their ministry as well. The objective is to keep a cool head in the midst of the storm. Failure of leaders is not the result of the difficult times in which they must lead, but how they respond to problems. Peter's perspective challenges postmodern church leaders to gain renewed balance and fresh perspective gleaned from the leaders primal beginnings. This reminder served them while they were engaged in their present service regardless of any precariously stressful situation they faced.

---

34   McKnight, 267.

THE SHEPHERD'S FORMATION

WHEN THINKING ABOUT THE FORMATIVE years of ministry, I am reminded not to despise diminutive beginnings. I served a small rural community in Western Kansas with a populace of two hundred and fifty. The greatest challenges were not presenting eloquent messages, holding funerals or weddings, or handling church administrative affairs, though these were important tasks, rather it was to believe that God would take care of our needs. Though a parsonage was provided, I paid utilities and a humble car payment on a salary of one hundred dollars a week in 1983. This provided my wife and me with twenty-five dollars weekly to live on and conduct church business. With no savings or other personal source of income, our faith was stretched from the get-go at this ministry.

My dad would ask how we made ends meet financially speaking. He believed I was mismanaging our money until he learned what our annual income was. He then commented that we weren't mismanaging it because there was nothing to manage. The only explanation he had aside from his personal disbelief was that God had to supply our needs.

I recall an instance when the cupboard was bare, and our modest resources were depleted. My wife inquired where our next meal would come from along with our next supply of groceries. The thought of not being able to provide for my home hit me hard, and yet I had worked as hard as any man in our community. I was not accustomed to a meager livelihood, having left a well-paying job prior to accepting our first charge. Holding her hand, I simply said, "Let's pray," and that we did. Dropping to our knees, we fervently prayed with seemingly unanswered results.

Suddenly, we were startled when the doorbell rang. I immediately sprang up to answer the door, and to my surprise no one was there. However, a huge box of groceries was at the threshold, filled to capacity. I hastily searched for a neighbor or anyone who was around the house to thank them for their generosity, yet I saw no one or even a vehicle in sight. We never discovered who made this timely delivery or its origin. But we knew it was the result of God's divine provision affirming His faithfulness.

Fortunately, we were blessed with a pioneer spirit that eagerly desired to please the Good Shepherd with little regard for selfish intent or gain. Overwhelmed with the joyful excitement of serving our charge seemed to cut the edge of disparity and need. Onlookers would have perceived us to be poor and without, yet we discovered satisfying fulfillment with wealth beyond the world's measure.

This was a time of personal discovery and spiritual formation that would give birth to a radical yet powerfully relevant faith accompanying us during the years of ministry to come. It didn't matter whether or not we were eating high on the hog or low on the bologna. Believing God to be responsible for our health and other sources of wealth initiated a way of life where we exercised our faith daily. This faith is the result of our initial reaction to God's mercy and grace received at salvation that continues to increase daily as we grow in Christ, learning to depend on Him. From start to finish of a Christian's life, the key that unlocks heaven's storehouse is faith.

The testimony of one's faithful witness of Christ will certainly be tested, yet through it all will prove to be a powerful asset and a great heritage in the Lord. One should not diminish humble beginnings, for they forge character and add wisdom through life experiences. These early years of formative growth and service establish the elder's credibility as one who has been proven in faith as well as experience.

Peter represents himself as ranking among his fellow elders and as a witness of the sufferings of Christ. He is one whose own spiritual formation will persevere with him until he soon shares in the glory to be revealed. "I appeal to you as a fellow elder," he says in 1 Peter 5:1. The formation of an elder begins with an effectual witness developing from an experience of real salvation. He reminds the other elders of their common experience of redemption in Christ that now fosters a fraternal bond of service. The use of the term "elder" was natural for the church to use, as it was used to designate leaders of the Jewish community within the Old Testament and New Testament.

> Originally the Hebrew zāqēn meant a "bearded one," or older member of a family and the term is used frequently in the Bible for those who are older in years. However, the term *elder* most frequently refers to the ruling head of the family or clan. In Jesus' day these were predominantly the aristocratic leaders of the Jewish patrician families. They served in local village councils and alongside the Pharisees and Sadducees in the Sanhedrin, the great council of the Jews in Jerusalem.[35]

The word elder referred to a man's standing in his years of faithfulness and service. The focus in the local church was that of a pastor, overseer, and shepherd whose duties were to administrate and serve the church. "The title *elders*, *presbuteroi*, 'presbyters', describes their status as seniors or leaders. 'Bishops' (*episkopoi*, 'overseers') and 'pastors' (*poim nes*, 'shepherds') seen in the early Church of the New Testament times to have been alternative names for those here called

---

35   G. R. Osborne, *Elder*. eds. J. B. Green, S. McKnight, and I. H. Marshall. *Dictionary of Jesus and the Gospels* (Downers Grove, Ill.: InterVarsity Press, 1992), 201.

'elders' ministry or responsibility."[36] Wiser older men of both Jewish and Greek cultures were bestowed places of honor in the church, and the church continued to practice this role of influential status. Elders had great responsibilities in their communities and were expected to be good examples for people to follow.

Elders were set apart and called by the Holy Spirit ("The Holy Spirit said, Set apart for me Barnabas and Saul for the work to which I have called them" Acts 13:2). Elders were appointed and made ordained officers ("Appoint elders in every town as I directed you" Titus 1:5). Elders were shepherds and had oversight of the flock of God ("To the elders among you … be shepherds of God's flock " 1 Peter 5:2–3). They held true to sound doctrine, guarding the sacred message and preaching the Word (Titus 1:9).

Elders served in healing ministry through prayer and anointing the sick ("Call the elders of the church to pray … and anoint him with oil " James 5:14). Elders had leading decision making roles in the Jerusalem Council with the apostles (Acts 16:4), and elders were those to whom Paul gave the offerings that had been taken for the Jerusalem Church during the famine (Acts 11:30).

> The exercise of the elder's leadership in the local church was Peter's main emphasis that rests on the unity of those who, as pilgrims (I Peter 1:1) and in suffering (I Peter 2:21; 4:12; 5:8), come together as living stones in a spiritual house (2:5 the metaphor of building expresses growth). They serve one another (4:10) with different gifts as a witness to the grace of God which is being revealed in them. In the process, the OT order of elders from the $q \ h \ l$ seems to have taken over (cf. 5:1). In all this, according to the eschatological terminology of shepherd and flock, Christ stands at the head as chief shepherd, i.e. as Messiah.[37]

---

36 Alan M. Stibbs, *The First Epistle General of Peter* (Grand Rapids, Mich.: Eerdman's, 1978), 165–166.

37 L. Coenen, *Church, Synagogue*, ed. Colin Brown. *New International Dictionary of New Testament Theology* ,vol. 1. (Grand Rapids, Mich.: Zondervan, 1986), 305.

Peter knew that Christ's sufferings for humanity were real, providing salvation for those who would believe and endure to the end. He then exhorted the elders to lead under the Messiah's directive, marching to the beat of His drum.

"For *who am also an elder*, RV has 'who am a fellow-elder' (Gk. *sumpresbuteros*). Peter does not give orders as an apostle, but with sympathetic fellow-feeling, as one called to similar responsibility to theirs, he encourages and urges them in devotion to duty."[38] As an elder called by God to minister to his flock, Peter identifies himself with fellow servants.

He leads his cohorts to serve their charges as he has, making himself equal with them through the lens of compassion, humility, and personal accountability laboring together. Speaking as a fellow elder not a superior, Peter further implies their authority over their flocks is based on service not power, position, prestige, or pedigree.

McKnight states that "when able leadership is present, following the lead of the elders is healthy and effective. Just as it is morally healthy for children to follow the good guidance of their parents, so it is spiritually satisfying and edifying for the churches to follow the guidance of the elders."[39] Peter's solidarity with those whom he exhorts yields personal understanding, making them aware that their call to church leadership is an extension of his own calling.

> He turns directly to them, instead of taking a stand on superior authority he prefers to appeal to them as one on their level. He is bringing them up, as it were, to his level, saying, 'Your task in your local congregation is the same in essence as mine in caring for the church more widely.' Thus he impresses upon them the significance and responsibility of their task in the church. He is appealing to them on the basis of the common task that they share.[40]

---

38 Stibbs, 166.
39 McKnight, 266.
40 Marshall, 161.

Peter is requiring these co-elders to do nothing less than what he would do. His primal initiative is to follow Christ completely. "When a Christian leader can stand up in all humility and ask others to follow as he or she follows Christ that leader is doing exactly what God has called (cf. I Cor. 11:1). Life is more important than office, just as it is true that our children learn more from what is caught than what is taught."[41] The implication is that nobody is better than anyone else, including leaders. We all are called to serve in the Master's vineyard, laborers together setting forth Christ's example to the world.

I remember when the issue of my personal calling came up in the most unlikely place. I had brought my fiancée home to introduce to the family over the holidays. At a huge annual Christmas party out in the country, we entered the big ole house with an inviting, warm fireplace. Children were playing everywhere, and most of the adults had gathered around the kitchen table sharing Christmas cheer. I don't know if it was all store-bought or homebrewed. My fiancé approached the kitchen, while they tried to conceal their Christmas beverages by holding them under the table or covering them with napkins due to a slight twinge of embarrassment.

They knew Mary's boy Steve was attending Bible school to become a preacher. Ironically, as I began to introduce Tammy, my Uncle Rufus questioned my ministerial vocation. He asked, "Are you store-bought or called?" He knew his grandfather, my great-grandfather, had been a God-called Southern Freewill Baptist minister out of the old school. I immediately responded, "I am called, of course. There are no price tags hanging on my soul for hire."

With a sigh of relief, the family began to greet us with open arms as always embarrassingly setting their beverages to the side. It is imperative for a person to know his calling an election sure, because at the end of

---

41   McKnight, 274.

the day it is all about the call that will keep one going onward. There is no substitute for the call of God.

Peter challenged his readers to catch the significance of their roles along with his. He embraces his calling as a leader in the church, a calling that will eventually lead him to his martyrdom. Leadership is often formed through fiery trials of suffering and persecution that forge impeccable character and integrity and develop an effective witness. Fire tempers metal for strength, and iron sharpens iron to obtain the cutting edge.

Peter recalls the incidents seen and personally experienced in our Lord's life becoming the guarantor of this testimony, which he calls "A witness of the sufferings of Christ." He saw the mockery, ridicule, and slander of Jesus. He knew how others had questioned and doubted Christ. The rejection, unbelief, and rebellion were still prevalent in his mind. He knew the blatant denials against the Lord's claims. He saw Christ suffer in the Garden of Gethsemane, the trials of humiliation accompanied with abusive beatings, and the crucifixion at Calvary.

The sufferings of Christ still burned in Peter's heart, a vivid picture he could never forget. He realized this imprint of suffering was complete, for Christ had risen with the hope of eternal glory. "Just as Christ's suffering is not an end in itself, but a means to a great end, namely, perfection (Heb. 2:10), so also is the case of his people (I Pet. 5:9). The essential goal for which the Christian suffers is that of the kingdom of God. Thus the Christian awaits not the *end* of suffering but its *goal*."[42]

Peter's pastoral appointment by the Chief Shepherd ("tend my sheep" John 21:16) "strengthens and confirms Peter's special position as an apostle, to which the Gospels bear witness (a position, however, by no means absolute or capable of being handed on). Peter's special responsibility is

---

42   B. Gärtner, *Shepherd*, ed. Colin Brown. *New International Dictionary of New Testament Theology*, vol. 3. (Grand Rapids, Mich.: Zondervan, 1986), 568.

to the whole flock, to the whole church."[43] He identifies with the elders' suffering, indicating that he not only proclaims Christ's sufferings but actively participates in them.

"But rejoice that you participate in the sufferings of Christ, so that you may be overjoyed when his glory is revealed" (1 Peter 4:13). When a shepherd and the people of God encounter Christ's sufferings, conflicts, and adversities, they must never forget who called them to serve in the first place. This simple assurance will enable God's people to endure and move forward in their Christian service paying whatever the price joyfully working in His service.

This brings to mind the story of Adoniram Judson, the famous missionary to Burma who never forgot who called him. He endured untold hardships trying to reach the lost for Christ, continuing with a missional focus despite suffering hunger and privation and being thrown into prison. Subjected to incredible mistreatment, he bore ugly marks made by the shackles and chains that bound him. "Undaunted, upon his release he asked permission to enter another province where he might resume preaching the gospel. The godless ruler indignantly denied his request, saying, my people are not fools enough to listen to anything a missionary might say, but I fear they might be impressed by your scars and turn to your religion!"[44]

At times church leadership has suffered grievously, however believers can honestly endure trials and not lose faith. This is more than historic truth, seeing current liberal ideology eroding biblical values and moral absolutes, for we do not know to what extent the modern shepherd may suffer. The truth of faith lies not in God's blessings, circumstances, or intellectual answers but in a revelation of God Himself. Believers are assured of God's presence in suffering when they attribute honor to Him

43   E. Beyreuther, *Shepherd*, ed. Colin Brown. *New International Dictionary of New Testament Theology*, vol. 3. (Grand Rapids, Mich.: Zondervan, 1986), 568.
44   P. Tan. *Encyclopedia of 7,700 Illustrations* (Rockville, Md.: Assurance Publishers, 1984), 1377.

and dare to do right no matter what or who goads them to do wrong. In so doing, a believer will allow honesty to be the guide, which helps alleviate some confusion while he or she suffers.

You'll never know what kind of trouble a day will bring in the life of a shepherd. On behalf of my church, I went to Haiti on a short-term mission tour. Haiti is place of civil unrest and very little law, where the national religion is Voodoo. It is also the poorest country in the western hemisphere. The annual income is three hundred and fifty dollars, and eighty percent of the population lives in abject poverty. Two-thirds of all Haitians depend on the agricultural sector.

The general poverty allows drug lords and gangs to escalate spreading their terror throughout the country. Haiti is also a major Caribbean transshipment point for cocaine en route to the United States and Europe, a fact which encourages substantial money-laundering activity. Additionally, Colombian narcotics traffickers favor Haiti for illicit financial transactions and pervasive corruption. However, these situations in Haiti also breed an opportunity to reach needy people with humanitarian, social, and spiritual help.

On a Saturday, a resident missionary, a national pastor, and I left the province of Thomassique, a rural mountain community not far from the Dominican border. After conducting a three-day crusade medical clinic and returning to Port-au-Prince, we were approaching the town of Hinche, a place known for its barbaric gang activity. Several months prior the gangs of Hinche killed a local police officer by decapitation, played football with his head and dragged his body up and down the road.

Quietly driving away from this town, our small band of mercenaries of grace approached a river crossing leading up to Goat Mountain, which is the main road back to Port-au-Prince. A gang of thugs assembled at the crossing had put together a makeshift barricade so they could collect a toll for their work on the road ahead. It's customary for some of the locals to remove fallen rocks in order to make the road usable. This was not the case on this road, as it was clear there had been no work done on this crude trail in this back country. This gangs well-planned robbery with eighteen armed Haitian men demanded payment for passage. They were all dressed in dark Nike sports apparel and trendy sunglasses. Completely different from the locals who barely could clothe themselves with tattered rags and worn-out sandals.

The resident missionary, an American female, stopped her jeep at the barricade. A spokesman for the gang staggered up to the jeep. It was evident he was intoxicated on the local rum and very unpredictable. The missionary gave the man five Haitian dollars to hopefully satisfy his demand, yet the thug insisted on more money and refused the small amount by throwing it back into the missionary's face.

In the process, the missionary told the spokesman in his native tongue, "You have stolen and plundered my people and God's children enough, no more, that's all I'll give you." The national pastor with us insisted she meet their demands, or we'd all be killed. At this point, the men at the barricade began to remove it, assuming she had met their demands. When the missionary saw a glimmer of an opening between the barricade and the river, she threw the jeep in gear and floored the gas until we had crossed the river and began to ascend Goat Mountain.

This situation was in accordance with the Haitian proverb, "Milk the white cow 'til she dries up." On this day, the gang lost their prized white cow and couldn't milk it any longer. This Haitian gang's holdup got stood up; hooray for the good guys! Perhaps our benevolent band of mercenaries of grace serves as an example in dealing with these thugs in life-threatening situations. It takes undaunted courage, a desire to do right, and a love for the Lord and the people we serve.

Faithful obedience is required without respect to our conditions in life. Do not look backward for blame but forward to what God is doing. When one is down, it is easy for him or her to play the blame game and point out the perspective assailants for your demise. Relationships can grow stronger through suffering without dragging others into our pit of despair. They may be the ones God will use to bring you up. Our loving Father does not want us to suffer and gives sufficient grace for our needs. God will bring you through suffering and trials as long as one holds on to faithful obedience. "Trust in the Lord with all your heart lean not to your own understanding" (Proverbs 3:5).

"Peter is intent to motivate church leadership that continues the witness of the apostles, whose testimony to the truth is indeed based on eyewitness experience."[45] Church leadership should not shun the hardships of the ministry but stay true to Christ's testimony.

> The courageous act of leading the church in perilous times rather than renouncing Christ is itself a form of witness that Peter shares with local church leadership. The apostle willingly embraces apostolic leadership of the church, making himself vulnerable to the same hostile forces that killed Jesus. Those who follow in the footsteps of Jesus (2:21) witness to the truth of his message as they share in the suffering of rejection he experienced. This construal of *martys* cohere well with the major theme of I Peter: all believers are called to suffer as necessary for their faithfulness to Christ.[46]

Peter was true to his call in serving Christ; he was willing to bear anything, knowing that the promise of heaven and the glory of life eternal are real. Peter's identification and participation is stated by the noted scholar Alan Stibbs: "*The glory that shall be revealed* is the glory divinely destined for God's Christ (i. 11), a glory given to Christ after His resurrection (i. 21), a glory yet to be openly revealed (cf. iv. 13), and a glory in which Christ's people, including Peter, are then to share as joint-heirs with Him (see Rom. viii. 17, 18)."[47] Unlike the fortune, fame, and glory embraced by Harrison Ford in the classic Hollywood *Indiana*

---

45   Jobes, 301.
46   Ibid, 302.
47   Stibbs, 167.

Jones films. The glory Peter refers to bears real significant implications to his readers.

Peter's reference to "the glory" is an expansion of the Old Testament idea of the word *ḵ bôd*. This term indicates the presence of God's glory in all His divine activity. The displaying of God's moral excellence to His creatures evokes their praise for what they see and for the benefits He brings and connects humanity with His presence. "In the NT glory means the divine-eschatological reality or manner of existence. Salvation lies in man and nature having a share in this manner of existence. The presence of this 'personal' *doxa* of God in Christ means the presence of salvation."[48]

Humanity's goal in all its members' actions must be God's glory in the sense of worship by word and deed. God so made us that we find the duty of worship to be our supreme delight, and in that way the furthering of our own highest good. Man's chief end is to glorify God, and to enjoy Him forever. "Glory" represents God's presence, displaying His divine purpose, power, providential care, and expressed love toward humanity.

"For the Greeks fame and glory were among the most important values in life. The rabbis also had a high esteem for a man's honor. Jesus stated in John 5:44 that seeking honor from men is incompatible with faith. The Christian's hope is 'the hope of glory.'"[49] Peter had personally experienced the eschatological glory in which the suffering church participated and now awaits the joy that is soon to come. Peter suggests Christ's suffering and the glory of life eternal are one in the same, two sides of a coin. He describes his present participation in suffering as a part that ensures the other half of the coin, where he is one who also shares in the glory about to be revealed.

---

48 S. Aalen, *Glory, Honour*, ed. Colin Brown. *New International Dictionary of New Testament Theology*, vol. 2. (Grand Rapids, Mich.: Zondervan, 1986), 47.

49 Ibid., 47.

The noted author Karen Jobes says, "[I]t is unlikely that the glory refers directly to the transfiguration or the resurrection of Christ."[50] Peter saw Christ's glory manifested, recalling experiences with the glorified Christ. The glory of Pentecost was deep in his soul as it was at the initial outpouring. Peter's heart passionately raced as he was assured of the Lord's return, anticipating a greater eternal glory with Him.

"What is significant here is that he expects this so vividly that he considers himself *already* to be a 'partaker' of that glory. Knowing that he is faithful now, he already anticipates his participation in what is coming. This should encourage his 'fellow-elders' to continue on the same road of witness and participation."[51] An assurance of a better day to come promotes continuance in the struggle, proliferating hope. This reminds one that there is a payday coming someday and it will be the Good Shepherd who passes out the checks.

Peter inspires the elders to embrace their calling "anticipating the promise in 5:4 that those who, like Peter; entrust themselves to God and continue to faithfully serve the church will receive the unfading (i.e., immortal) crown of glory when Jesus appears."[52] Only a relevant deep-seated experience with God can keep one's focus on remaining true to the end while serving faithfully.

---

50 Jobes, 302.
51 Peter H. Davids. *The First Epistle of Peter* (Grand Rapids, Mich.: Eerdmans, 1990), 177.
52 Jobes, 302.

THE SHEPHERD'S PRACTICE

SIGNIFICANT INSIGHT TO THE SHEPHERD'S practice is found in Peter's charge "Be shepherds of God's flock that is under your care" (1 Peter 5:2). The word "shepherd" is used as a verb in the aorist tense, active voice, and imperative mood with the meaning of "to tend, guide, or guard." Pastors are shepherds of the local flock with the intention to oversee, feed, and care for the spiritual needs of the congregation.

"The word *shepherd* in Hebrew means a feeder. The primary concern of the pastor, as the term is used here, is thus not to direct the affairs of the church, but to teach them. And the pastor-teacher's task is to explain it and make it easier for the people to understand, assimilate, and apply it."[53] Peter suggests the shepherd's job is to feed the flock by virtue of his office through preaching and teaching. The good food that has been so diligently prepared is, of course, the Word of God. A pastor will commit a huge proportion of time, resources, and energy to rightly divide the Word, delivering good news to humanity. The way in which we treat the Word of God is the way we treat God, and the way God will treat us. It is imperative that the purveyor of Scripture wisely engage the consistent practice of hermeneutics in preparation.

---

53   Stanley M. Horton, *What the Bible Says about the Holy Spirit* (Springfield, Mo.: Gospel Publishing House, 2005), 269.

In his *Dictionary of Hermeneutics*, James D. Hernando defines hermeneutics as: "The discipline that studies the theory, principles, and methods used to interpret texts, especially ancient ones such as the sacred Scriptures. Traditional hermeneutics focuses primarily on the discovery of the historical meaning as intended by the author and understood by the original audience. Modern approaches to hermeneutics often stress the role of the reader in creatively engaging the text in the discovery of its Significance for today."[54]

Christian interpreters share many hermeneutical principles and methods in common with those who expound other kinds of literature. By terming the Bible "spiritual," we affirm the role of the Holy Spirit who applies its message to readers. With the Spirit's aid, we explore the Scriptures and find life-giving and life-changing meaning. As we respond in faithful obedience, we grow in maturity; we worship and praise the God of the Bible. The Spirit-energized reading of the Scriptures gives direction to our thought and guidance to our lives.

That which motivates and produces purpose for an individual is due to an individual's existing assumptions about the world. It is these personal presuppositions that help us create the interpretative process. The art of Biblical interpretation demands that a person deal first with his personal thoughts of the subject matter, weighing them out on the scale of intellectual honesty. Sound faith and understanding is derived from one's presuppositions, which in turn lead us to decide how we will eventually interpret the Scriptures.

Presuppositions authorize the execution of disciplines requiring rules and principles as a guide to weed out assumptions that may not be in line with a Scriptural text and also to defend the presuppositions that are at the core of our faith. The discipline of hermeneutics gives balance and integrity to the assumptions that are formulated in one's thought

---

54 James D. Hernando, *Dictionary of Hermeneutics* (Springfield, Mo.: Gospel Publishing House, 2005), 23.

process, giving credibility to the revealed Word of God, manifesting itself in the thoughts and hearts of men where presuppositions are born.

The Bible is God's Word, and the Holy Spirit speaks through it. It follows from the first presupposition that the Bible is reliable and true. It is divine revelation through which God speaks, so the Bible possesses ultimate authority. For this reason, it must constitute the standard for all human belief and behavior. It speaks truthfully about who we are and how we are to live, so rejecting the message of the Bible means rejecting the will of God. What God says must be true, for God cannot lie nor will He mislead.

Modern religious pluralism has fabricated for itself a "me-first" mystic culture with the viewpoint that right can be wrong and wrong can be right awaiting one's opinion. There are no established absolutes with religious pluralism because religious pluralism fuses various religions and cults, whipping up a blend of religion that allows anything to be regardless of how depraved or unreligious it may be. Pluralism endorses no absolutes or moral values which are found in Biblical reference, thereby creating spiritual apathy.

The impact of this belief system upon fundamental evangelical churches is an attack of a pluralistic philosophy proliferating biblical illiterates in the church, therefore allowing biblical understanding to be thrown to the wind. When this thought is received by many nominal church members, a rapid decline in sound doctrine and spiritual maturity is foreseeable. Refuting religious pluralism has to begin with faith in the God of the Bible and knowing His word is truth.

God's eternal truth establishes absolutes and standards that have begun with Him by the revelation of His written word. The use of right biblical interpretation should be a mandate to properly divide the Word of truth, correctly informing and empowering the church with

God's authoritative revelation. God will do His work in building the church if spiritual leaders will do due diligence to the message.

The Bible's unity provides the authoritative foundation for Christian faith and practice; this has been the historic Christian perspective. Readers synchronized apparent contradictions within the Bible, or resorted to typology, allegory, or the principle of the *regula fidei* ("the rule of faith") to interpret complex texts in the light of clearer ones. Yet an acknowledgement of the Bible's diversity allows interpreters to appreciate each text, book, and author on its own terms, as a result distinguishing what God intended to say to his people at each point in their history. Scripture's unity helps define what the Christian faith, in contrast to alternatives; its diversity reminds the church that different expressions of that faith may have a claim to legitimacy.

The Bible presents a clear message to anyone willing to read it, and that is why people throughout history have understood its teachings. Its depth exhausts the human mind, for it draws from God himself and deals with the most important and urgent issues of human existence, now and eternally. The Bible is written so that common people can catch its truth. The central message speaks plainly to human hearts, even after scores of superseding centuries.

In John Wycliffe's *On the Pastoral Office*, a challenge pertaining to the status of a pastor resounds. "Now there are two things which pertain to the status to pastor: the holiness of the pastor and the wholesomeness of his teaching. He ought to be holy, so strong in every sort of virtue that he would rather desert every kind of human intercourse, all the temporal things of this world, even mortal life itself, before he would sinfully depart from the truth of Christ."[55] Though he was condemned as a heretic, the later English reformers hailed him as a hero of the faith for translating the Bible into English. Wycliffe's labor exemplifies a shepherd's practice

---

55   William C. Placher, *Readings in the History of Christian Theology. Vol. 1.* (Louisville, Ky.: Westminster Press, 1988). 185.

to deliver truth in its purest form, allowing access for all to receive no matter the cost.

The shepherd's focus needs to be on the Lord, on applying himself in Christ's powerful work feeding the flock. Under God's authority the shepherd is commissioned to rightly divide and distribute the wonderful words of life. He does not seek to give pleasure to nor take delight in tickling the ears of the fold. The goal is not to entice people for favors or fame but to please only the Lord. The shepherd proves that the food provided is palatable and passes FDA approval, the Father's Divine Authority.

Ignatius, the early church father and bishop of Antioch in Syria, encouraged the Christian churches to "use only Christian food. Keep off foreign fare, by which I mean heresy. For those people mingle Jesus Christ with their teachings just to gain your confidence under false pretenses. It is as if they were giving a deadly poison mixed with honey and wine, with the result that the unsuspecting victim gladly accepts it and drinks down death with fatal pleasure."[56]

The preacher is the purveyor of spiritual truth and the conduit through which it is conveyed to the people. Not to be confused with void, slick talkers or lighthearted empty expressions but wholesome truths, solid soul food that is relevant and spiritually conceived. The goal of feeding is to spiritually refresh the flock, enabling a strong walk derived from the Divine source of nourishment. The results are that all who come to Christ will be allowed to experience positive discipleship by teaching them to observe all the things that Jesus has commanded.

The pastors were called upon to look after the flocks as under-shepherds of Christ by way of His example as the chief shepherd. As a metaphor for spiritual realities, people could relate easily with a shepherd's occupation. Shepherds were the guides, providers, protectors,

---

56   Placher, 16.

and constant companions of sheep. They are inseparable from their flocks, even though the work is lonely, challenging and periodically life threatening.

The term "shepherd" is an Old Testament metaphor wherein the Lord holds the leaders of Israel responsible for failing to care for the flock they were overseeing (Ezekiel 34:1–10). This text is a critical rebuke to the selfish and unreliable leaders who cared more for themselves than their charges.

They were consequently held accountable to God and removed from their post and livelihood. Out of this situation comes the promise of a shepherd from the line of David who will truly love and care for the flock (Ezekiel 34:23). "Yahweh is described as the shepherd of Israel in Hosea 4:16: 'Will Yahweh now feed them as a lamb … ' The Old Testament metaphor implies that Israel is God's possession and that it can yield itself with full confidence to the guidance, provision and help of its Shepherd."[57]

> In the NT the shepherd metaphor is used to delineate how pastors and elders should fill their office. When Jesus restores Peter, he uses the imagery of feeding and tending a flock to designate Peter's apostolic and pastoral task (Jn. 21.15-17). Elders in the church are encouraged to watch carefully over themselves and the flocks entrusted to them and are warned about those who would seek to ravage it (Acts 20.28-29). These elders are also admonished to perform their pastoral task willingly, out of a genuine desire to serve rather than for monetary reward, and to focus on being examples to the flock instead of rulers over it (I Pet. 5:3-4).[58]

---

57   J. Jeremias, *The Palestinian Shepherd. Theological Dictionary of the New Testament*, vol. 6. Ed. G. Kittel, G. W. Bromiley & G. Friedrich (electronic ed.). (Grand Rapids, Mich.: Eerdmans, 1976), 499.

58   L. Ryken, J. Wilhoit, T. Longman, C. Duriez, D. Penney, and D. G. Reid, ed., *Sheep, Shepherd* In *Dictionary of Biblical Imagery* (electronic ed.). (Downers Grove, Ill.: InterVarsity Press, 2000), 783.

The image of shepherding the flock is practical to congregational leadership. The elders' duty in relation to the flock is connected with many severe personal hardships and public endangerments. In spite of its challenges, the shepherd leads and tends the sheep. "Rooted in the sheep-shepherd relationship, the biblical imagery stresses the care and compassion of the divine shepherd and the dependence of people on God to meet all their needs."[59]

God loves His people as His own and sees to it that they are nourished, protected, and given the best care possible. He feeds the sheep, even if He has to pick them up in his arms and carry them to the pasture (Isaiah 40:11). He guides them away from rough and dangerous terrain (Psalm 23:1–4). He seeks out and saves the lost sheep (Matthew 18:11–12). He keeps them separate from the goats (Matthew 25:32–33). He protects them with the sacrifice of His own life (Jn. 10:11). He restores the wayward sheep and brings them back (1 Peter 2:25). He rewards the obedient and faithful sheep (1 Peter 5:4).

Without the shepherd, the sheep would be endangered, wandering about getting lost and never finding the way to true life. Those without the shepherd of God receive no food, no inspiration of soul, and do not satisfy their inner hopes for peace, love, and joy. Without the shepherd, the beasts, the temptations, and the trials of the world would seek to destroy all who wander about. The shepherd was to willingly serve his flock with eagerness and become the example for the sheep to follow.

The directive to the elders in 1 Peter 5:2 is forcefully depicted using clear imagery:

> The image of a "shepherd" is that of a concerned guide, not of a severe ruler (although the image of shepherds had been applied to rulers in parts of the ancient Near East). Charges of illegitimate gain were often made against moral teachers in the ancient world, and it was necessary for Christians to avoid even the appearance of

---

59   Ryken, Wilhoit, Longman, Duriez, Penney, and Reid, 783.

impropriety. (Like certain officials in the Jewish community, these Christian leaders distributed the funds for the poor).[60]

The meaning tending the flock carries the purpose of performing the duties of a shepherd. In sum, the shepherd's practice was to feed, guide, seek, save, protect, restore, reward, and keep the sheep that are entrusted in his care at all coast.

The German theologian, Leonard Goppelt says, "The commission of the elders is expressed, first of all, in v. 2a in the same language as in Acts 20:28 ("...Be shepherds of the church of God"), and the promise with which the directive for the elders closes in v. 4 uses the same language as Acts 20:32, though "inheritance" is promised there, while here what is promised is "the garland of glory."[61] The author Peter Davids points out, "[T]he command to elders to shepherd is found only here and in Acts 20:28-29. Both places significantly connect shepherding with 'watching over it,' showing the shepherding is a job of oversight."[62] The shepherd's job of overseeing is more than management and maintenance mode. This individual should strive to practice and exemplify true qualities of biblical leadership in order to effectively lead the flock.

---

60   Keener, 720–721.
61   Leonhard Goppelt, *A Commentary on I Peter* (Grand Rapids, MI: Eerdmans, 1993), 338.
62   Davids, 178.

SHEPHERD'S BIBLICAL LEADERSHIP

"LEADERSHIP IS LEADERSHIP, NO MATTER where you go or what you do. Technology marches forward. Cultures vary from place to place. But the true primal principles of leadership are constant—whether you're looking at the citizens of ancient Greece, the Hebrews in the Old Testament, the armies of the last two hundred years, the rulers of modern Europe, the pastors in local churches, or, the business people of today's global economy. Leadership principles stand the test of time."[63]

A person in leadership should be one who has the ability to persuade others to take action that is in accord with the leader's purposes or the shared purposes of all concerned. The late Tom Landry, a successful and well-known football coach, described leadership as getting grown men to do what they don't want to do and like it. According to John Maxwell and other authorities on leadership, they imply that leadership is influence; nothing more, nothing less. Obviously, each definition contains some insight, yet each falls short in some respect, especially when we consider spiritual leadership.

Biblical leadership is, in fact, being willing to deny self, follow God, and minister to people. Throughout the history of humankind, God has used men and women to advance his redemptive plan and to lead people in the way they should go by word and example. Several

---

63 John C. Maxwell, *The 21 Irrefutable Laws of Leadership* (Nashville, Tenn.: Nelson, 1998). Introduction, xx.

examples of a leader include a captain, chief, commander, conductor, guide, and shepherd. While these descriptive metaphors illustrate certain roles of leadership, a common thread intertwines each one, which is influence.

People die. Yet their influence doesn't. Cain brutally murdered his brother Abel and buried him to silence his lips and erase any memory of him, but he couldn't do it. The Bible says in Hebrews 11:4 "He [Abel] being dead yet speaketh." Cain couldn't dig a grave deep enough and wide enough to snuff out his brother's influence once and forever. You can embalm a body and carry it away in a hearse but you can't do the same to influence. Influence is what we leave behind. It can be bad or good, and we must remember that it cannot be turned on and off at will. It sticks with us like our shadow, going everywhere we go.

The right influence can help bypass the pitfalls of bad decisions. What you decide today will determine your destiny tomorrow. For little decisions can make huge differences in our lives. A slight nudge of influence can give one the courage to make the right decision.

Influence can challenge small-mildness to think big. Far too often we aim too low and are willing to settle for far less than God has in store. God wants you to be a lender not a borrower; a warrior not a weak whippersnapper; gem not a gaffe; and a dignitary not a donut hole. May the right influence inspire you to think big and realize that you can never put a strain on God's ability?

Influence inspires one to be bold. Timidity is like a tramp bellying up to the bar at closing time hoping for a handout and often getting none. Boldness on the other hand is assertiveness in action and demands that will not be denied. God said it in these words: "Let us come BOLDLY to the throne of grace … that we may … find grace to help in time of need" (Hebrews 4:16).

The Old Testament gives the contemporary leader insight into the role and importance the Spirit of God had on the various leaders of

Israel. The Holy Spirit gave chosen ones knowledge, understanding, and special enabling power to lead God's people in the way He desired for them while experiencing the miraculous power which was beyond their own personal ability.

Authority was given by God to those of His choosing for the purpose of leading Israel to fulfill His plans. It has been through charismatic leadership that the kingdom has both been established and promoted on Earth. The individuals God has chosen to guide his people in the direction they should go were not particularly special individuals but were most often ordinary people called and endowed by the Spirit of God to perform special and extraordinary tasks.

"Responsible godly leadership involves submission and homage before God, the divine Sovereign, and humble modeling of covenant righteousness before His people in accord with His will and for their good."[64] Character of this nature is noted in many of the Old Testament leaders. An excellent example is Moses, the first great leader of the Hebrew people.

As the leader of God's people, Moses was instructed to perform miracles before Pharaoh and to request the people's release. Through a series of ten miraculous plagues, Yahweh did indeed crush the Egyptians and liberate the Hebrews from slavery. The deliverance from Pharaoh and the miraculous crossing of the Red Sea marked only the beginning of the Israelites' arduous journey to the Promised Land led by Moses. Though Moses experienced great difficulty and frustration, he was equipped, empowered, and sustained in his task by the Spirit of God.

It was not Moses' natural abilities, giftedness, or intelligence that allowed him to lead God's people in such an effective manner, rather it was the Spirit of God that enabled and empowered him to perform the tasks God called him to do. What qualified Moses for this kind

---

64   Daniel I. Block, The Burden of Leadership: *The Mosaic Paradigm of Kingship* (Bibliotheca Sacra Jul./Sept. 2005), 258.

of leadership role? Moses was chosen and called of the Lord. He was obedient and faithful to lead God's people in spite of the many hardships they faced. Moses' gifted abilities to perform the supernatural for Israel's exodus hinged on the very promise of God and His desired will.

The New Testament reveals Christ anointed and empowered by the Spirit of God. The Holy Spirit rested upon Him that He might do the works His Father sent Him to do. It was the Spirit of the Lord God that enabled Christ to preach good tidings and to perform miracles among the people. The Messiah, through the anointing of the Spirit of God, would demonstrate "servant-leadership" by serving others. In fact, Jesus said of Himself, "the Son of Man did not come to be served, but to serve, and to give his life as a ransom for many" (Matthew 20:26). His leadership style was not to "lord it over others," rather it was to "serve" others. This is a novel idea for today's church leadership.

At the inauguration of Jesus' ministry, at His baptism in water by John the Baptist, God declared, "the heaven was opened, and the Holy Ghost descended in a bodily shape like a dove upon him, and a voice came from heaven, which said, Thou art my beloved Son; in thee I am well-pleased" (Luke 3:21, 22, KJV). Luke states that Jesus was endowed by the Spirit of God for the mission He was to carry out (Luke 3:22, 4:17–21). Following Jesus' temptation, He "returned to Galilee in the power of the Spirit" and began performing miracles and promoting the kingdom (Luke 4:14).

The "servant-leadership" style Jesus modeled was in great contrast to that of the previous leadership of Israel. His Spirit-filled life and ministry became a pattern for not only His disciples but to all future leaders in the kingdom of God. Jesus spent His time on Earth instructing, mentoring, modeling, and giving the disciples authority to do the works He was doing through the Holy Spirit.

It was the Spirit of God which enabled the Early Church leaders to experience boldness to give witness to the cause of Christ in a hostile world. Leaders of the postmodern church must be courageously relevant to effectively reach this culture for Christ enabled by the Holy Spirit himself. Stepping outside the proverbial box, out of your comfort zone, is a deliberate challenge of self-interest. The impact made from this courageous step will greatly enhance your circle of influence and ability to lead. However, it will take more than the latest techniques to attract those not yet reached.

The relationship between leadership and the Spirit of God was the difference in leaders having strong witness and supernatural signs following as opposed to working in their own might and meager efforts. Leaders of today must realize true biblical leadership depends first and foremost on the knowledge, understanding, wisdom, and power that come from God. "It is not by might, nor by power, but by my Spirit, saith the Lord" (Zechariah 4:6).

The definition of leadership is having the office or position of a leader, or the capacity to lead, indicating this person with this position or capacity has commanding authority or influence. It implies that an individual brings to the table skill, superiority, and/or supremacy. There is no universally accepted definition of leadership in action, however. Why? Leadership is not a science, it is an art. Art, by its very nature, virtually defies definition. However, there are some very experienced people who have tendered some descriptions of leadership that I would like to mention.

Scholars Warren Bennis and Burt Namus say, "Leadership is ... doing the right things." Garry Wills states, "Leadership is mobilizing others toward a goal shared by the leader and followers. Vance Packard says, "Leadership is getting others to want to do something that you are convinced should be done." And J. Oswald Sanders says, most profoundly,

"Leadership is influence."[65] The person who strives to do the right thing ultimately is concerned to utilize his or her sphere of influence in recruiting a team specifically to reach an objective for a successful purpose.

In his book *Man at the Top*, Richard Wolfe states that leadership is "a man or woman taking leadership methods and skills God has given them, and dedicating it for the use and glory of God the Father. When God creates a leader he is given volition for action. God gives him the capacity to make things happen." It is in this way God works in and through people (Philippians 2:13).

"A Christian leader is someone who is called by God to lead; leads with and through Christlike character, and demonstrates the functional competencies that permit effective leadership to take place."[66] The attributes of moral fiber and intestinal fortitude define the true nature of an individual. Skills one attains through teaching or experiential learning enhance and prove to be of additional value in the development of leadership skills. The more a leader imitates Christ through practical daily life, the more he allows the Holy Spirit to refine his true character.

What makes a Christian leader? George Barna, in his book *Leaders on Leadership*, mentions three qualities that make a Christian leader. First, a leader is called by God for the specific purpose to lead. "The majority of humankind is followers. Those who have been anointed by him to lead are most valuable to the kingdom and the body of believers – in functional terms – by their willingness to follow their call and do that which followers so desperately need."[67] Their followers need to confidently know the leader's personal response with Christ is one that allows for a deep-seated desire to fulfill His will and not a personal agenda.

The second quality that makes a leader is exemplifying Christlike character. "Because the central function of a leader is to enable people

---

65   George Barna, *Leaders on Leadership* (Ventura, Calif.: Regal, 1997), 21.
66   Ibid., 21.
67   Barna, 24.

to know, love and serve God with their entire hearts, minds, souls and strength, the leader must himself possess the kind of personal attributes, characteristics of the heart, manifested through speech and behavior, that reflect the nature of our God."[68] The intent is to ensure Christ is vividly exalted so others may have opportunity to experience His gracious relevant life in real time.

The third quality of a Christian leader is that he acquires serviceable capabilities that allow him to perform tasks and guide people toward bringing about God's will. These are talents that receive fruitful awareness because they inspire people, directing their energy and wherewithal through team building, vision, entrusting authority to others, making resolute choices, strategizing, and accepting accountability for end results.

Leadership in the postmodern church must meet the challenges of its culture just as each generation of past leaders has. As much as any other time in history "the church of the twenty-first century needs missional thinkers and apostolic leadership. By missional leadership, I mean leaders who can read the Scriptures with fresh eyes, relating the story of redemption to the human condition in its present cultural contexts, contexts that are increasingly multicultural and influenced by global trends."[69] Business cannot continue as usual, just because we've always done what we do in the same old manner. A lot of good organizations have lost out, falling behind due to archaic traditionalized methodology and refusing a fresh look for a new approach.

"Leadership is not the private reserve of a few charismatic men and women. It is a process ordinary people use when they are bringing forth the best from themselves and others. Leadership is your capacity to guide others to places they have never been before."[70] In other words, leadership

68 Ibid, 24.
69 Eddie Gibbs. *Leadership Next: Changing Leaders in a Changing Culture* (Downers Grove, Ill.: InterVarsity, 2005), 25.
70 Gibbs, 26.

must be relational. No one person has a monopoly in this arena nor is it an exclusive club barring all others from joining. Leaders must develop relationships with people to influence the thoughts, behaviors, and beliefs or values of another person. They cannot and must not operate in isolation or vacuum.

A personal friend served twenty-five years leading the financial-aid department of a now major university. Upon his retirement one of the foremost banks in America hired him within the first week of his departure. The main leadership values he brought to the table were relationship skills and the ability of passing these skills on to his colleagues. The power brokers of the world recognize the worth of individuals that can develop and foster relationships adding towards their corporate successful future. How much more ought the church to invest in one of its greatest values that of relationship building between God, man and our world?

> "Leaders of today must focus on ministry by the church in the world rather than ministry in the church that is largely confined to the existing members. If the church is to carry out its commission faithfully, it must draw its models, inspiration, motivation and wisdom from the earthly ministry of Jesus in relation to His Father and the Holy Spirit. At the heart of Jesus' mission was the training of a group of close followers who learned by listening to his teaching, observing his interactions with people from all walks of life and working under his personal supervision. They were first disciplined learners before they were sent out as his personal representatives."[71]

Leadership knows what to do next and understanding the goal and the appropriate resources for optimally achieving it. Confusion can arise out of a misconception between leadership and management. Leadership connects with the top-line mentality and is involved in doing the right things. However, management is often bottom line mentality in focus,

---

71   Ibid., 31.

seeing how to accomplish certain tasks. It primarily seeks to do things right.

There are different styles of leadership, and knowing your style can effectively work for or against you. There are leaders who are driven by popular opinion, which leads to a consensus style. Another style is coercion, meaning that a leader drives individuals by force or compulsion. Leading by convenience creates an easy way out mentality, leading to the path of least resistance. This is one who just does whatever the majority of the people she or he leads ask of them. A caustic or cowardly leader is driven by the fear factor of change, which will also take a minimum risk factor. This leader rules by convincing people that change is scary and risky, therefore something best not pursued. However, a shepherd's leadership ought to be one of conviction. Conviction is driven by a strong belief in what should and could be done to make things better and more effective.

A principle rule to remember about leadership is that such a position may be given, but respect must be earned. The avenue in gaining this respect begins with fairness, integrity, and honesty. Respect for the dignity of every individual is a must while executing patience and encouragement. Denoting the difference in serving and being a servant will foster a servant attitude, ensuring quality and excellence through servant leadership.

There are basic elements of developing leadership. The first is knowledge—knowing what needs to be done and why. The second is skill—knowing how to do it. Where a leader's natural skills and abilities are deficient, they can be strengthened through training and equipping with the right tools. The third basic element is passion or motivation. The want-to in one's spirit is the factor that determines if a real desire exists to excel. Real leaders will strive to capitalize on strengths and manage around weaknesses while teaming up with others who get their passionate visions.

THE SHEPHERD'S ROLE

THE PRIMAL ROLE IN SHEPHERDING is servitude. "Serving as overseers—not because you must, but because you are willing, as God wants you to be; not greedy for money, but eager to serve; not lording it over those entrusted to you, but being examples to the flock" (1 Peter 5:2b-3). The role of the shepherd is grounded in servant leadership. "Peter describes how the *presbyteroi* are to shepherd the flock of God. The adverbial participle 'overseeing' (*episkopountes*), which modifies the verb 'shepherd' (*poimanate*), is then further qualified by three sets of opposing adverbial qualifiers."[72] The shepherds oversee with willingness not coercion, are not greedy but eager to serve, and are not domineering but lead by examples.

The servant-leader model common to the modern shepherd is the existence of a superior to serve and a task of service to complete. Servants are called to have a different attitude to their superiors, to seek their benefit rather than a self-seeking, self-serving attitude. Those that are served have the responsibility to care for and protect their servants. Peter wrote, "Servants, be submissive to your masters with all respect" (1 Peter 2:18, RSV).

Technically, a servant was to keep a low profile and status that varies depending on the situation and the status of the master. The quality of

---

72   Jobes, 304.

a servant most frequently referred to in Scripture is faithfulness. The apostle Paul commented that "It is required in stewards, that a man be found faithful" (1 Corinthians 4:2).

It is interesting to note the transfer from the concept of human servant to that of servant of God. Service of God is expected from all believers, but because of God's magnificent greatness, those who give special service are considered worthy of the title "servant of God" or "servant of the Lord" and are particularly revered and given high status. Servant leadership is unselfish. It refuses to rest on the inherent power of a position and desires to empower and release others for ministry.

Jesus expresses a significant truth in the very act of submission and servant leadership by the washing of the disciples, feet showing how to lead by example. Christ submits to the place of a slave taking his outer garment off to gird Himself with a towel in order to serve his followers. "The Greek word for 'the towel' with which our Lord girded Himself occurs also in rabbinic writings, to denote the towel used in washing and at baths. Such girding was the common mark of a slave, by whom the service of foot-washing was ordinarily performed"[73]

Jesus arose from His meal and took upon Himself the attire and position of a slave, as He was being none other than the supreme example of the servant described in Isaiah's prophecy whose purpose was to "pour out his soul unto death" (Isaiah 53:12). "He laid aside his garments even as He was to 'lay aside' His life. He tied a slave's apron round Him, poured water into a basin, and proceeded to wash His disciples' feet and wipe them clean with the towel, the outward badge of His servitude"[74]

Peter, not understanding the full significance of Jesus' act, objects to the washing of feet by the master. When Jesus told Peter, "If I do not wash you, you will have no part with me," he quickly responds

73 Alfred Edersheim, *The Life and Times of Jesus the Messiah* (Grand Rapids, Mich.: Eerdman's, 1980), 501.
74 R. V. G. Tasker, M.A., B.D., *The Gospel According to St. John* (Grand Rapids, Mich.: Eerdman's, 1978), 155.

offering to be washed all over. "If I do not wash you … mean that the question is not simply one of washing, but a question of who does the washing. Peter must participate in the work of Jesus (13:8–9). He lacks a cleansing that only Jesus can supply"[75] Peter may have thought that if a foot-washing would grant him inheritance with Jesus, he assumed his whole body needed washing. The spiritual cleansing work of Jesus on the cross portrayed by foot-washing is complete and no longer need be pursued. Rather, leaders must only to follow Christ's example of love, submission, and servitude.

While at an interview with a church board, I was asked sarcastically, "Do you practice foot-washing?" Denoting a prideful arrogance, I immediately responded, "Do we need to?" and thus ended that segment of the interview with an uncomfortable yet thought-provoking transition. Though we may no longer implement the practice of foot-washing on a regular basis, the spirit and example Christ exhibited needs to be followed in order to live an effective Christian life of humble servitude.

When Jesus had finished washing the disciples' feet, He put on His outer garment and sat down with them. Having transitioned from the role of a slave to that of the teacher, Christ now questions His apprentices. "Know ye what I have done to you," he says. "You are correct in calling me Master and Lord." Yet the teacher had done what the lowliest servant would normally do. Jesus spoke of servantship not rulership that would keep their relationship together. The Lord's ways are vastly different than humanity's and can only be in sync with someone when his or her will is submissive to His.

I received a valuable lesson early in the ministry about rule and success. I struggled to get ahead and succeed in the ministry using my position and authority. Then through prayer, I had a Holy Spirit moment. The Spirit prompted me saying the Father's will was not in the stepping

---

75 Gary M. Burge, *John the NIV Application Commentary* (Grand Rapids, Mich.: Eerdman's, 2000), 369.

up of the proverbial ladder of success, but to step in His will, no matter how humbling doing so may be.

I realized true humility is simply seeing oneself in the light of God's will with a grateful heart for His providential care, and that staying in the Father's will is true success. Jesus is our example of true humility and gives us His command in John 13:14: "ye also ought to wash one another's feet." This command resonates with a loving service to be exhibited among His followers. Jesus concludes by telling the disciples that true humility and service are to be paramount.

Christ continues His dialogue with the disciples, saying "that no servant is greater than his master, nor is the messenger greater than the one who sent him." Here he reinforces the concept portrayed by foot-washing that none should consider himself above others, and what applies to the master would also apply to His servants. "Jesus now wants his followers to exemplify that same love to one another. His act of sacrifice cannot be repeated, but his model of self-giving love can become a natural feature of the community that follows him and imitates him (13:14–15). Later, Jesus will say that our love for one another should be like his in yet another way: We may be called to lay down our lives for our friends (15:12–13)"[76]

First, servant leadership in the church should be conducted with the proper intent of personal willingness and a sense of divine calling, not a sense of internal or external coercion. Servant leadership focuses on the needs and growth of those being led, not the needs of those who are leading. Jesus told his disciples, "Whoever desires to become great among you; let him be your servant. And whoever desires to be first among you let him be your slave — just as the Son of Man did not come to be served, but to serve " (Matthew 20:26–28). A pastor's view of his role as an overseer needs to have a positive motivation to accomplish pastoral ministry. "In Judaism the volunteer was a person who placed himself

---

76   Burge, 371.

at God's disposal, either in terms of military service (Judg. 5:2, 9) or of sacrifice (Ps. 54:6). Thus also in Northern Asia Minor the elders are to act voluntarily, for that is what it means to act 'in a godly manner.' After all, none of God's acts for humanity was done out of necessity, but voluntarily, out of grace."[77]

There have been shepherds called to feed the flock of God who refused to serve for the right reasons as their hearts held them back due to the cost or required sacrifice. Some called were not willing to serve for the reproach of the ministry would be unbearable for them. Their duties, expectations, and demands were too constraining. Church leadership that is inappropriately motivated is not to be offered to God. The intent of begrudging service will never please God, only offend Him.

When the intent of service is properly grounded, the servant has a ready mind, a forward spirit, and more than a willingness—rather a zeal—to serve. Shepherds must oversee the flock in a way that gathers (harvests), pastures (feeds), and defends the Christian community so it may thrive in the midst of social pressures. "Ministry should not be an unwanted burden; pastors are not to serve out of a sense of false guilt or fear, or in an attempt to please people. Any of these attitudes or motives can lead to unwillingness to shepherd or to shepherd in an inappropriate manner."[78]

Second, the pastor of a flock is not to be motivated by greed for financial gain but have a spirit of enthusiasm to serve others. Peter justly presents the warning against greed. The elders were often in charge of the church's purse, and were frequently given financial earnings for their support. Elders could turn to greed, expecting a better income for their service, justifying their gain which Peter condemns. Leaders also could have been enticed to misuse the funds for personal benefit.

---

77 Davids, 179.
78 Max Anders, *Holman New Testament Commentary* (Nashville, Tenn.: Broadman & Holman Publishers, 1999), 89.

In a rural Midwest church where finances were not the best and pastoral support slim, a huge temptation came to my attention. The town drunk who had stumbled into our services on a few occasions showed up at my door with an intriguing offer that would test the resolve of my integrity. He possessed a large wad of rolled bills over three inches in diameter with good size denominational value. He asked if I would like to receive his tithe from the money he had just won gambling. Boy, how I would have liked to receive that sizeable amount of money, knowing our present financial need. Yet something did not resonate in my spirit. I didn't think it was the right thing to do.

After several minutes of coercing me to take his money, he backed down and said, "I didn't think your integrity would allow you to take my sin money." Then he left. Later he attended a Sunday service sober and miraculously got saved. Not long after he donated time and resources to build a nice marquee for the church, which exceeded the amount he tried to offer me. In retrospect, I thought it was a good thing I didn't take his gambling money out of greed or even personal need and instead allowed God to take care of us His way.

> The NT is critically opposed to the normal economic orientation of profit in so far as profit is looked for out of selfish motives. Titus 1:11 is directed against teachers of false doctrine from Crete who were spreading abroad ideas with an eye to their own advantage. They teach "for base gain" (cf. also the warnings to the leaders and deacons of the congregation in I Tim. 3:8; Tit. 1:17; I Pet. 5:2). Anyone who is out for gain and whose view of life is dominated by the profit-motive falls into an arrogant self-centeredness, and thus into sin (James 4:13).[79]

A pastor should not take oversight of the flock for personal profit and gain but out of right intent. The misconceptions of the ministry as a mere

---

79   B. Siede, κερδοσ (kerdos), ed. Colin Brown. *New International Dictionary of New Testament Theology*, vol. 3. (Grand Rapids, Mich.: Zondervan, 1986), 137.

profession, a means of livelihood, a way to serve humanity, possessing giftedness, and a means of providing misguided encouragement of others can cause people to go into the ministry for the wrong reasons. No one should ever enter the ministry for reasons that usually accompany the work. Peter said in Mark 10:28, "We have left everything to follow you!" suggesting unselfish motives to serve Christ. The pastor must know with assurance the gilt-edge promise of the Lord that if he seeks first the kingdom of God all these (material) things will be added to him. He is to practice the lesson of Phil.4:10–19: to be content in whatsoever state he is in.

Third, the servant-leader's right attitude is his eagerness to give and not the desire to take. Anders says, "*Eager* is a strong term meaning 'with enthusiasm, with energy and excitement.' This is certainly difficult when facing the attacks of Satan and when one is attempting to lead a church through a maze of suffering and persecution. At the same time, it is an indispensable characteristic for pastor-leaders to model."[80] This statement is not to insinuate that pastors never get downhearted or lose their zeal. It does describe a whole manner in which they shepherd. Without this innate desire to serve faithfully, pastors have failed, spiraling toward an injurious approach to ministry.

Selfish gain of wealth and material possessions is a type of man in the garden of Eden reaching out after the illegal fruit not content with the abundance made available. This attitude often indicates an ungrateful heart and degenerative spirit that is no longer thankful unto the Lord for provisions in life. The excess of love of money brings selfish division between God and those who have personal vested interest. Eventually a person who is possessed by the excessive craving of monetary gain inherits alienation from God and others.

"*Finally*, they are to serve 'not by domineering ... but by being examples.' Jesus had clearly pointed out that the way of the world at

---

80   Anders, 89.

large was for leaders to domineer over the led, expecting obedience and the 'perks' of leadership. His disciples were to be servants, not bosses; ministers, not executives."[81] Peter advises a model of leadership that opposes local churches being dominated by their leaders. The words "those entrusted to you" in verse three suggest that the shepherds speak to the flock as to how to conduct their lives and administer discipline when necessary. When this is done in a self-serving manner, elders abuse their position.

The hunger for power is as prevalent and addictive today as it was in the first century. Power-seeking shepherds pursue their own agendas and pollute the very plan of God for personal prestige, power, or financial gain. In doing so, they strive to increase their own rapport and lead by dominating the flock with intimidation.

Given current trends of corruption, many Christians have been desensitized and are no longer surprised or embarrassed by corrupt leadership in our serving institutions, including government, education, businesses, or religious organizations. The actions of those in authority are questioned, and suspicion lurks over those who are power brokers. Leadership is no longer isolated to an office, but is achieved though the conduct of trust and respect which has to be earned and maintained.

No Christian leader in his or her right spirit plans to disavow the prescribed practice of servant leadership exemplified by Jesus, nor predetermine to deliberately dictatorially control from the perspective of a religious hierarchy. However, due to the lack of a diligently guarding their motives, many leaders have forsaken their principles thus leading them down a slippery slope, damaging themselves and those they serve. A breakdown of leadership occurs when priorities shift from an external focus to an inward focus, which can harm the welfare of any church. A church growth consultant once told me that in most average-size congregations, one could pick out generally one or two yard bosses who

---

81   Davids, 180.

may lead due to wrong motives, thereby keeping the kingdom from growing.

The general editor of the Holman New Testament Commentary on 1 & 2 Peter, Max Anders's analysis of 5:3 states, "Lording it over the people in a congregation is not the same as leading people in the congregation. The words *leading* and *lording* should not be confused because they are distinctively separate in meaning and tone. 'Lording it over' people means to rule forcefully. It is a word of harshness that implies excessive use of authority."[82]

Pastors should not lord over the people, meaning they should not behave in high-handed, heady, or dictatorial ways. Rather, they should be an example for others in the community to follow. "The desire to be a leader rather than one who is led is strong in many of us. Fair enough, high is the danger of *lording it over* other people and failing to show them proper respect. This attitude, typical of worldly rulers, was condemned by Jesus (Mk. 19:42), who warned his disciples not to emulate the world's ways."[83]

Shepherds are to lead with a mutual respect and trust reciprocated by the flock. This rapport is not always a given and usually has to be earned. People often place confidence in those who labor in their presence gaining influence due to an exemplar life. Peter Davids states "Being an example fits well with the image of 'flock,' for the ancient shepherd did not drive his sheep, but walked in front of them and called them to follow."[84] This is a call to humbly serve others in genuine love and honor preferring one another (Romans 12:10).

A pastor should not delight in the use of authority (although at times he must exercise it), nor should he seek to increase, preserve, or flaunt his authority. This characterizes leadership that has degenerated

---

82   Anders, 90.
83   Marshall, 163.
84   Davids, 181.

into dictatorship. Godly leadership in the church that can serve as examples to the flock involves sensitivity to peoples' needs, affection for people, and authenticity of life, an enthusiastic affirmation, without deception, greed, flattery, or authoritarianism.[85]

The right perspective on authority within the framework of the church assures the local shepherd that he is not laboring without an ever-watchful eye. The great shepherd superintends His flock and directs the under-shepherds to carry out His will. The realization of Christ's supremacy over His church instills a very humbling servant spirit that will keep in check the times when leaders experience selfish, dominating desires. Under the Lord's authority are callings and gifts distributed freely to the fold, leaving no room for personal gain or glory.

---

85   Anders, 90.

THE SHEPHERD'S REWARD

"AND WHEN THE CHIEF SHEPHERD appears, you will receive the crown of glory that will never fade away" (1 Peter 5:4). The shepherd's reward is now and yet to come. The faithful shepherds of God's flock who willingly and eagerly serve as role models will receive the unfading crown of glory when Christ, the chief shepherd is revealed. "The *archipoimenos* was the overseer of the shepherds when a flock was too large to be attended well by one. The *presbyteroi* are not simply to follow the example of Christ as independent agents when shepherding God's people; instead, they are to recognize themselves as underlings of Christ the Chief Shepherd, to whom they will be held responsible."[86]

Jesus is characterized in the Scriptures as the true shepherd in four different perspectives. "Jesus refers to himself as the 'good shepherd' who 'lays down his life for the sheep' (John 10:1–29). Jesus is called 'the great shepherd of the sheep' (Heb. 13:20), the 'Shepherd and Guardian of your souls' (I Pet. 2:25), and 'the chief Shepherd' (I Pet. 5:4)."[87] First, Jesus identifies Himself as the Good Shepherd who "lays down His life for the sheep" (John 10:11). The Lord's passionate desire to save lost humanity compelled Him to be constrained to the cross. Jesus as the Good Shepherd brings "into focus his office as shepherd in all its uniqueness, in contrast to

---

86 Jobes, 306.
87 Gerald L. Mattingly, *Shepherd*. Ed. P. J. Achtemeier, P. Harper & Row. *Harper's Bible Dictionary,* 1st ed. (San Francisco, Calf.: Harper & Row, 1985), 942.

contemporary false claims to the office of shepherd and to the shepherd-gods of antiquity. He is the good, the lawful shepherd, because he opposes the wolf at the risk and at the cost of his life."[88] Despite all the attacks the people of God have incurred throughout the ages, Jesus will continue to defend against demoniac influences who strive to assault His pearl of great price.

The second characterization of the true shepherd is that Jesus is called the great Shepherd. "May the God of peace, who through the blood of the eternal covenant brought back from the dead our Lord Jesus, that great Shepherd of the sheep, equip you with everything good for doing his will, and may he work in us what is pleasing to him, through Jesus Christ, to whom be glory forever and ever. Amen" (Hebrews 13:20–21). Verse 20 refers to the resurrection with regard to the exaltation of Christ in his glorified state. The resurrection of Jesus Christ is undeniably anchored in the evidence of His post-resurrection appearances pointing to the promised reward of an eternal body. We are promised a spiritually real incorruptible body in place of our now corruptible one. Grant Jeffery, The author of *Heaven the Last Frontier* states,

> "The clearest indication we have of our future body was shown in the resurrection of Jesus Christ. He appeared to His disciples and His followers on many occasions during the forty days after He rose from the grave. He specifically promised us that in the resurrection, our body would be like His body. He knew the tendency of humans to assume the life after death would be some eerie ghost-like existence. He taught us the reality of our heavenly body."[89]

The gospel writers give detailed accounts of those who saw Jesus physically, yet emphasize His exaltation and glorification. These who witnessed Jesus having endured the horrific events of His passion, death,

---

88   Beyreuther, 568.
89   Grant R. Jeffrey, *Heaven The Last Frontier* (Canada: Frontier Research Publications, 1990), 45.

and burial now see Him as He appears in their presence. The newly hewed, slightly used empty tomb where the corpse of the Lord was laid, now vacant with the stone rolled back is strong evidence for the resurrection. Here the natural and the unnatural are oddly merged together.

Obviously, the stone was not rolled back for the benefit of the risen Savior but for those who attest to the resurrection. When Jesus arose, He was in His resurrected body, the spiritual body of the spiritual dimension having no physical boundaries. He did not need the stone rolled back to leave the tomb because spiritual substance has no bearing on material substance. Yet the witnesses needed to enter the tomb and see the truth for themselves. John's gospel gives accurate testimony of the risen Savior.

John's account of the post-resurrection appearances of Christ begins in 20:11–18 when Jesus reveals Himself to Mary of Magdala in the early morning hour, probably about seven a.m. Mary being distraught at the thought that someone had removed the body of Jesus turns her eyes away from the tomb and sees a person whom she assumes is a gardener. Not recognizing the Master, Mary has her first dialogue with the resurrected Lord. Jesus asks her, "Woman why are you weeping and whom are you looking for?" Mary asked of Christ whom she supposes is the gardener, and replies "Where have you put him?"

In some of the resurrection narratives Jesus is not immediately recognizable by his friends. In the story of the two disciples on the Emmaus road, for example, 'their eyes were kept from recognizing him' (Luke 24:16). Mary, however, may simply have been so blinded by her tears that she could only make out the form of a man standing behind her. But the kindly words in which the supposed gardener addressed he encouraged her to think that now at last she had found someone who could tell her what had happened to the body of her Lord.[90]

90   F.F. Bruce, D.D., F.B.A., *The Gospel of John* (Grand Rapids, Mich.: Eerdmans, 1983), 388

But Jesus "calling her by name was all that was necessary. Immediately her distress vanished; here was something far better than she had dreamed possible. Instead of the dead body she had hoped to recover, she found herself face to face with her living Lord."[91] Mary excited at the site of her Lord reaches out as to embrace Him, yet He admonishes her in the present tense to stop clinging to Him. She was not to waste time doing that. Instead, Jesus commissioned her to run and tell of her great discovery to the disciples.

The next appearance of Jesus according to John is later in the first day of the week after He had appeared to Mary at the tomb (20:19–25). Mary had passed on the message that the Lord had commissioned her. The disciples are assembled behind locked doors that may keep out the spying eyes of Jewish neighbors and authorities. We know from (20:24) that Thomas was not with the disciples when Jesus came that evening. The locked doors could not keep Jesus from His beloved followers. He came and stood among them and said, "Peace be with you." "[T]hese words are far more than a greeting.

"At a profoundly personal level, Jesus is summing up the essence of his work and presence in the world. Peace is the gift of his kingdom. In 14:27 and 16:33 Jesus promised that this peace would be his gift to them; now he has delivered it."[92] "Jesus' sudden appearance to His disciples behind locked doors, like His emergence from the tomb, demonstrated that in His resurrected state He was no longer bound by earthly limitations."[93] Jesus commissions His ambassadors by saying "as the Father has sent me, I am sending you."

The time for the apostles to be sent has now arrived. "The technical term 'apostle' is avoided by John, but by the use of the cognate verb *apostell* he indicates that the disciples now become effective apostles in

---

91   Ibid., 389
92   Burge, 558.
93   Colin G. Kruse, *The Gospel According to John* (Grand Rapids, Mich.: Eerdmans, 2003), 380.

the sense of 'sent ones'. The Son's mission in the world is entrusted to them, since he is returning to the Father; but as the Son had received the Spirit in unrestricted fullness for the discharge of his own mission (John 1:32–24; 3:34)."[94] The disciples now receive the Spirit in order to carry out their newly received mission. At this point Jesus breathes on them, imparting the Spirit to endow them with power for ministry, designating a divine role for them to declare it is God who effectively remits or retains sins.

John records another appearance of Jesus in 20:26: "after eight days his disciples were again inside and Thomas was with them." Thomas undoubtedly was at fault and faithless, and his unbelief was inexcusable. The disciples who had proclaimed the truth to him were not liars, nor could they have all been deceived. Thomas just refused to believe them, acting intellectually superior and demanding physical evidence of the Lord. The doors once again being shut and locked, Jesus makes his entrance as He stands in their midst giving them the greeting 'Peace be with you' (20:26). This visit is twofold, not only allowing Thomas to have a firsthand physical appearance of the risen Christ, but for Jesus to give a much greater reason for all who have not been privileged to experience the Lord and His glorified body as His disciples did.

> Jesus does not disparage the faith of Thomas ("So *now* you believe because you see me?"), but simply cites a fact ("Because you have seen me, you have believed"). Thomas's faith is anchored to sight. Then Jesus goes on to utter a blessing not on those who see and believe — which is certainly a virtue paraded throughout the chapters of the Gospel. Rather, he offers a blessing on those who believe but have *not seen*. Jesus points forward beyond Thomas, beyond the apostolic circle, to the world of the church, to believers who come to faith through the testimony of the apostles.[95]

94   Bruce, 391.
95   Burge, 563.

The confession of Thomas saying 'my Lord, my God' of 20:28 is one of the greatest confessions recorded in the Bible. Thomas dropping to his knees, having all doubt dispelled is now confronted and convicted by Jesus' sudden appearance. Christ knew of Thomas' unbelief and used the same words as Thomas demanded: 'Reach hither thy finger, and behold my hands; and reach hither thy hand, and thrust it into my side: and be not faithless, but believing' (20:27).

With the confession of Thomas, the writer now clearly presents the statement of purpose for the book of John (v. 30–31). The many signs Jesus did probably refer to the signs in the gospel, highlighting seven miracles Jesus performed. Beginning with the miracle of Cana, turning water into wine (2:1–11); the raising of the royal official's son (4:46 –54); healing the lame man at the pool of Bethesda (5:1–9); the feeding of the five thousand (9:1–7); and the raising of Lazarus from the dead (11:1–44).

These signs were not all that Jesus did, as He performed many others not recorded in this book. "The expression many other signs may also include other appearances of the *risen* Jesus which this evangelist has left unrecorded. Christian faith, to strengthen which was the primary purpose for which the Gospel is stated to have been written, rests on the conviction that *Jesus is the Christ, the Son of God;* and is the source of eternal life which is the possession of the Christian."[96]

Jesus is seen having breakfast by the Sea of Galilee with His disciples (John 21:1–23), and this is the third time Jesus appeared to His disciples after the resurrection (v. 14). 'There were together Simon Peter, and Thomas called Didymus, and Nathanael of Cana in Galilee, and the sons of Zebedee, and two other of his disciples. Simon Peter saith unto them, I go fishing. They say unto him, we also come with thee. They went forth, and entered into the boat; and that night they took nothing' (v. 2).

---

96   R.V.G. Tasker, M.A., B.D., *The Gospel According to St. John* (Grand Rapids, Mich.: Wm. B. Eerdmans Publishing Company, 1978), 227.

After a night's work of fishing proving unprofitable, the morning begins to break. The disciples see a person just like they would see anyone standing on the seashore. They have no thoughts of a vision, hallucination, or spirit. To them there is nothing strange about a person standing on the shore. This individual shouts from the shore, "Have you caught any fish?" The answer is a resounding no from these weary fishermen.

The familiar voice from the shore speaks with authority, telling the fishermen to throw their nets to the other side. When they do, they catch one hundred and fifty-three fish. Jesus having supernatural knowledge knew where the fish were and used this occasion to teach that He is the risen Lord, and the same Lord who took care of His disciples before the crucifixion. He would continue to take care of them, but there was one significant truth they needed to learn. The resurrection increased His care and added much more to their salvation. He is the risen, sovereign majesty of the universe able to provide all things for His own (Matthew 6:25–34).

John is the first to recognize this voice as belonging to the Master. Peter proceeds by tying his outer garment to himself and diving into the water to reach the Lord. Jesus has set fish grilling on warm coals and has bread ready to eat. When the disciples approach Jesus, they remain apprehensive. They know Him, yet something is quite unusual, even otherworldly about him now. This unfamiliarity prompts these devoted followers to silently ask, 'Who are you? Yet none of the disciples dared to ask Him' (v. 12).

Of our present experience of the risen Christ Albert Scheitzer wrote, in a well-known passage: 'He comes to us as One unknown, without a name, as of old.' And those disciples, although they saw him then (as we do not now) with outward vision, experienced something of the same kind: they knew him quite well, and yet in a sense they saw him as a stranger, one who henceforth belonged to another order

71

of existence. But he put them at their ease, inviting them to come and share the breakfast which he had prepared for them. The bread and the fish represented the harvest of the earth and the harvest of the sea.[97]

The disciples knew it was the Lord who had appeared unto them. In human terms, it was not possible; a dead man arising from the grave was impossible. The physical and material world knew nothing but corruption, decay, sin, and death. Yet, Jesus was sitting and eating with them. He had conquered death, hell, and the grave and returned to life again. They knew just what Jesus wanted them to know, and that is the reality of His resurrected body, His sovereign majesty, and the careful provision made for them in conquering death (John 11:25–26).

Peter is given a new commission in verses 15–17 by the challenge brought forth from Christ: 'feed my sheep'. This passage is important for the church and its ministers, because it notes that the lesson of love is essential for ministry. After the meal, the disciples sat and chatted with one another. Jesus may have already had a private conversation with Peter regarding his denial and assured him of his full restoration (1 Corinthians 15:4–5). All the disciples knew of Peter's denial and the Lord's challenge to him will serve to reinforce his leadership, making sure Peter would not deny his Lord again or cease in the mission he was about to accept. The Lord taught the disciples that not even the greatest among them could ever serve Him and bear godly fruit unless he loved the flock of God.

Three times Peter was commissioned to feed and tend the flock of God. Jesus called Peter by his full name, reminding him that he was the son of Jonas of humble beginnings and a lowly father. All that Peter had and would become was of God, and he was nothing apart from Christ, and nothing apart from the mission he was about to receive. How many

---

97   Bruce, 402.

people would have more life, purpose, meaning, and significance if they would surrender to Christ? If Peter really loved the Lord, then he would accept the commission to be a shepherd of the flock of God.

It would take Peter's total commitment, requiring him to follow the leadership of the Holy Spirit. "When first he was called from his occupation of catching fish to be a follower of Jesus, he was told that thenceforth he would catch men (Luke 5:10; cf. Mark 1:17). Now to the evangelist's hook there is added the pastor's crook, so that, as had often been said, Peter proceeded to fulfill his double commission 'by hook and by crook'."[98] When Peter was young and before he knew Christ, he girded himself, dressed, and walked where he willed. He was able to live and do what he wanted when he wanted. Accepting this call, he no longer could live his life as he wished. Now his Savior and Lord would direct his path.

> Such good shepherds are not people whose ministry promotes ego and personal glory, who disguise their own ambitions in pursuits of "excellence" in so-called great churches and institutions (ministries, denominations, colleges, or mission agencies). These are not people whose competitiveness harms other shepherds, who always look over their shoulder to see if someone else will enjoy a parallel glory. These are men and women who simply hear Jesus' words, "Follow me," and obey, thinking about their own discipleship more than that of others.[99]

Peter's dialogue with the Lord shifts to his friend and colleague John who is following them, and he asks what of the beloved disciple (21:20–23). It was obvious that Peter and John were close, and Peter's interest in John's work and future was genuine and probably came naturally.

The Lord told Peter that his business was to follow Him and remain faithful to his personal calling. Peter was not to focus on another man's

---

98   Bruce, 405.
99   Burge, 600.

call or ministry. Jesus challenged and called Peter again by saying "Follow me" in verse 22.

The Master may have wanted Peter and his servants to understand that Peter should not be distracted or desiring of other people's ministries. That he need not copy, conform to, or meddle in something that he was not about. The Master was molding Peter into a vessel of honor for His service, not to be tainted with the likes of something He did not want. Total commitment demanded that all Peter's energy and efforts would be placed in the service of the Lord's call upon his life. The plans Jesus had for His beloved disciple was not necessary for Peter to know.

Christ's appearances testify to the fact of His resurrection and glorified body. "For that record still comes home to us with the self-authenticating quality of eternal truth. He to whom this witness is borne is the revelation of God in human life, and then he is received, God dwells in us and we in God."[100] The present time continues to testify to Christ's resurrection as His witnesses continue to flourish and follow after the Master. "Blessed are those who have not seen and yet have believed" (John 20:29).

Just think of the newly created spiritual body complete with our own uniqueness still possessing the original nature and imprint with which God has endowed us. "Our individual D.N.A. cellular structure is uniquely different from the other six billion people alive today. The same awesome, intelligent God who designed our natural body with such particular care for diversity and identity has also designed a heavenly body for us to live in forever."[101]

The third characterization of the true shepherd is that Jesus is identified as the shepherd of our souls "For you were like sheep going astray, but now you have returned to the Shepherd and Overseer of your souls" (1 Peter 2:25). This indicates the shepherd welcomes His wayward children with open arms. He exemplifies selfless service moved

100 Bruce, 410.
101 Jeffrey, 44.

by compassion for the lost. He is the guardian of our souls, giving loving oversight and shouldering the responsibility willfully.

Jesus continues to pull at the heartstrings of men in order to draw them unto to salvation. It is not His will that any should perish, but that all will have everlasting life. "The soul, as the part of us which believes and is sanctified, is destined to an inheritance in God's future kingdom. Thus here the contrast is not between spirit, soul and body, but between the soul and the lusts of the flesh. It is souls in this sense that are meant in I Peter 2:25."[102]

The fourth characterization of the true shepherd is seen in 1 Peter 5:4, where Jesus is referred to as "the Chief Shepherd": "And when the Chief Shepherd appears, you will receive the crown of glory that will never fade away." He has direct oversight of the people of God and will appear returning to the world with great glory, rewarding the faithful. "When the Chief Shepherd appears, he will naturally pay his under-shepherds. The term 'receive' is often used for receiving pay or wages. In our context, as often in the NT, the pay is the eschatological reward (Eph. 6:8; Col. 3:25; Heb. 10:36), which stands over against the temporal gain for which elders are not to be greedy."[103]

Peter encourages the pastors to persevere in their service during trying times. Shepherds should desire to serve God regardless of the cost. They realize their positions as under-shepherds serving only temporarily in Christ with a goal of increasing His Lordship. The victory is sure and set in the eschatological mode for the imminent return of our Lord as Peter promotes this event in the hearts of his fellow servants. Christ's return adds hope to their desperate situations and encourages their faith to be steadfast and firm, living for the moment when Christ returns.

The image of Christ's returning with "the crown of glory that will never fade" in 1 Peter 5:4 bears reference to 1 Peter 1:4 regarding "an

---

102 G. Harder, *Soul*, ed. Colin Brown. vol. 3 of *New International Dictionary of New Testament Theology*, vol. 3. (Grand Rapids, Mich.: Zondervan, 1986), 685.
103 Davids, 181.

inheritance that can never perish, spoil, or fade." "The phrase *a crown of glory* means not just 'a glorious crown', but a share in glory as one's reward."[104] The inheritance of eternal life from God comes with abundant rewards.

The believer's new nature is a reward consisting of being made blameless by possessing a wholehearted devotion in doing the will of God "so that you may become blameless and pure, children of God without fault in a crooked and depraved generation, in which you shine like stars in the universe" (Philippians 2:15). The new nature will provide a glorious body fit to live eternally with God (1 Corinthians 15:42–44). The believer's nature will be attired in white robes before the throne of God (Revelation 7:9--12); joyously sharing His rule over many things (Matthew 25:23).

God assures additional wealth and rewards to His heirs. The blessings of the Lord bring wealth without trouble (Proverbs 10:22). He will give crowns of rewards to the faithful. For example a crown of incorruption that will last forever (1 Corinthians 9:25). A crown of righteousness rewards the righteous and is given justly by the righteous Judge (2 Timothy 4:8). A crown of life indicates the victor's reward for the faithful believer who endures to the end (James 1:12). A crown of glory is awarded by the chief shepherd for faithful servants (1 Peter 5:4).

The crown that Christ will reward His under-shepherds is drawn from an image well known to the first-century Greco-Roman world. "*Stephanos* in the NT is often the prize of athletic victory as a metaphor for the eternal reward of the faithful. The eternal hope is set against the transience of perishable wreaths (I Cor. 9:25; I Pet. 5:4): in the former case there may be allusion to the use of *withered* parsley for the crown at the Isthmian Games."[105] The wreath of leaves that would soon fade away was placed on the heads of those who won athletic games.

---

104 Stibbs, 168.
105 C. J. Hemer, *Crown, Sceptre, Rod*, ed. Colin Brown. *New International Dictionary of New Testament Theology*, vol. 1. (Grand Rapids, Mich.: Zondervan, 1986), 406.

In contrast, the victory attained through perseverance until Christ is revealed is presented in these books as an unfading, everlasting glory that will remain with His shepherds who were true to the faith. This is an incentive for the local pastor to continue his race no matter how hard the struggle may be. Some shepherds may want to faint while striving to do their best, yet only notice others' success and temporal rewards with little or no recognition for their own efforts. Encouragement comes from Galatians 6:9: "Let us not to be weary in well doing: for in due season we shall reap, if we faint not." A good thought to keep in mind is that faithful consistent service will always bring forth its due rewards as the Good Shepherd is keeping the records.

Personal Paraphrase of 1 Peter 5:1–4:

To the pastors of the churches in Asia Minor I plead with you as a fellow pastor who has personally seen Christ's sufferings and now look to the glory that is yet to be seen. Be pastors of your churches that are entrusted to you, serving in leadership not because of wayward compulsions, but because you desire freely of your own will as God desires this of you. Be not motivated by personal gain, but be ready to serve not being high-handed or dictatorial over those in your care. But be somebody that others will want to follow after. When Jesus, the ultimate Good Pastor arrives, you will receive as a reward an eternal crown that will always be with you.

Moral Application

CONTEMPORARY SIGNIFICANCE EXTENDS THE PRINCIPLES of pastoral growth, administering fairness in leadership, developing the right attitude, and leading by example to fulfill the mission of the church. Practical relevance pours out from Scripture calling for a grassroots theology to be investigated and applied. Scriptures state, "As every man hath received the gift, so minister the same one to another, as good stewards of the manifold grace of God" (1 Peter 4:10). God's grace is revealed in many ways through the life of a shepherd.

A misnomer appears to subsist using the term pastoral theology. A study of God is theology, and pastoral theology would be better identified as the pastor's personal study of God from a pastoral perspective. Though not so euphonious, a better terminology than pastoral theology would be the knowledge of pastoral work which applies to the study of the art and science of being a pastor. Moral and practical applications stand out in many phases of a pastor's work and responsibilities.

God's message to the postmodern pastor to shepherd the flock has moral application for church leadership, providing a checklist of proper and improper pastoral motives. Pastoral leadership of the church is required to guarantee the survival of the flock in difficult, troubling times and leading forward in good times. The success or failure of a community of faith is largely dependent on the way in which its leadership is exercised. Godly leadership in the church provides patterns to the flock involving authenticity of life, affection for others, and sensitivity to their needs.

PASTOR'S GROWTH

THERE MUST BE A GROUNDBREAKING growth process starting with a seed of formation for pastoral leadership to thrive. This primal seed is an effectual witness resulting from a bona fide experience of salvation. I recall my own personal salvation encounter. I grew up in an un-churched home. My father was a salesman and professional musician who played his music through the country western circuit—in other words, he was a honky-tonk man. My mom was a seamstress who worked various jobs for many years. Most Sundays we spent time at home relaxing or traveling to the country for family visits. I remember in my youth, occasionally watching the *Gospel Jubilee* and Oral Roberts on an old black and white Zenith. My dad enjoyed watching these gospel entertainers while they opened my eyes to a whole new world. When Reverend Roberts would give the invitation to be saved or healed, I would lay my hands on the TV despite occasional ridicule from my dad. But I knew something was up with this Jesus who was lifted up by means of the old black and white picture tube.

As I grew, I felt an awareness of my sins, though I thought I was a morally good person. I knew my life was not what it ought to be, sensing a void inside. I was reared with the belief of God by the example of a widow, who lived with our family and cared for us children, but I knew I was not right with God. While attending church services with this woman, I responded to an altar call when the invitation was given and received Christ as my Lord and Savior. For the first time in my life I was free of guilt and bondage caused by sin. My next step was to follow the Lord by water baptism. It wasn't long that I became aware of a deepening hunger for God and received a full blessing of the Holy Spirit.

My spiritual life began to form in the fire of His presence. In order for me to personally understand the blessing experience known as the baptism of the Holy Spirit, I waded through a lot of backward, misdirected ways of thinking. I had bought into the concept that those Pentecostals hung from chandeliers, acted like drunks, spoke in goofy languages, rolled around on the floor, and were just plain weird. My mom even advised me to stay away from those kind of people. It then occurred to me that Pentecostal folks acted a lot like my family out in the country around the Fourth of July after sampling too much of the recipe jar, though without the chandelier. Why, I oughta feel right at home.

I realized that for every real deal in life, the Devil, the dark enemy in our soul, has a copy or falsehood to baffle and belittle the truth. This influence did not keep me from attending the Pentecostal church. Yes, this magnificent, beautiful edifice had the grandest of chandeliers I had ever seen, yet not one person could even reach its crystals in order to swing. One Thursday evening, the church presented a unique youth service with emphasis on the Holy Spirit. At the altar call, my friends began to have wonderful experiences of this blessing. Yet as fervent as I tried, I got nothing.

Several weeks later after prayerful seeking, I found myself at the altar again praying and seeking an endowment of God's presence, power, and purpose. Right then a huge hand spanned my whole head and gently laid on me. I realized it was one of the players of the World Football League that was now headquartered in Birmingham. He began to agree with me in prayer. I was not oblivious to my surroundings or unconscious in any way, just the opposite.

I began to experience a heightened sensitivity to the presence of the Spirit of God, accompanied by a wonderful peace in my soul. Sensing His presence, I yielded my faculties while remaining very cognizant. There came forth a manifestation of heavenly speech as the Holy Spirit Himself gave utterance. It was nothing that I had done; I was only open and receptive of a gift.

The blessing continues to add confidence and assurance, even in dark hours of trial and tribulation. He truly abides with His people. A heartfelt hunger for God and burden to reach the lost bound by a strong conviction to preach the gospel convinced me of the call of God on my life. Holy fire now consumed my innermost desires with divine purpose.

The formation of a shepherd is initiated by a call to humbly enter into servant-leadership at the request of Christ. A shepherd serves a lowly position tending the sheep. This is what Jesus requested of Peter when he told him to "Feed my sheep." The shepherd's position was tagged with disdain and derision, making it a position that many would normally run away from. Tending sheep was not a life of fame and glory; it meant living a lonely life in the outskirts of communities and the backwoods away from the ivory-walled and gilded palaces.

Answering the call to "Feed my sheep" takes a bold, courageous leap of faith that is willing to follow Christ at any cost. The call to preach is a spiritual association. One of those things unregenerate persons do not understand yet is very real to the saved. The call is to take the never-changing message into an ever-changing world by adapting and not compromising the message and to be living personifications of this message in a culturally relevant way to society. Servant-leaders are not to isolate themselves from those who are in darkness. There will always be those workers of evil surrounding the light, be it the meth dealer, the alcoholic, family abuser, prostitute, or plain-old mean, corrupt people. We are called to penetrate this darkness in the light of God's love, participating in His divine nature (2 Peter 1:4).

The call to go to the darkness is our commission. In order for the lost to see the light, they must be able to understand it. Many people will not leave their comfortable zones, unwilling to connect to God given their diverse cultural backgrounds. The acceptance of becoming the perimeter of light is left to our willful choice as individuals and a collective body. The callings of God are all related to the realization of Christ's kingdom. The assurance that God initiated the call is vital, as it brings forth conviction that gives any believer endurance during times of trouble or setbacks. The callings of believers are means of accomplishing God's mission rather than having a sense of personal fulfillment or recognition.

I recall a time when the Lord reaffirmed the call personally to me. When I was a second-semester freshman discouraged and starting to question God's call and purpose, assurance came from an unlikely source. During an informal nightly gathering for prayer, a student from Kenya spoke a timely challenge to me. We were not closely acquainted, yet his words still echo in my soul. In his native African-British brogue he said, "Do you love me, Steve"? After the third time of saying this he followed up with, "If so, then feed my sheep." I knew the Lord used this brother in the faith to affirm the call to serve. This became one of those God moments that quicken in your spirit an unequivocal assurance of God's will and direction.

A pastor's training is vital to his formation. It is important to have the right spiritual influences that will eventually lead to an effective ministry. Peter presented himself as a fellow elder, and yet by virtue of his apostolic office he was a leader of the church enabled to impart spiritual guidance to his co-laborers. It is vital that a pastor is linked with mentors who can assist in his spiritual formation.

Peter's mentor was none other than Christ Himself who nurtured and trained His disciples, developing them into the leaders they became. When a person mentors others, that individual's labor develops expediently and continually. It is a great honor to pass onward the things of God which have been entrusted to you as you assist others in pursuit of their calling.

In a self-absorbed society, imparting what one has learned can be a very demanding and time-consuming task. The mentor must devote his time to younger servants who are eager to learn as doing so will become an extended continuation of the fruits of his labors, paying off huge dividends within the kingdom of God. Mentors' influence sets precedence spiritually, practically imparting suppositions of a worldview that lay the groundwork for ministerial service through growth presently and in years to come.

Networking with other pastors with whom the shepherd shares common interests serves as a source of encouragement, comfort, aid, and resources that contribute to renewal. To foster relationships with your cohorts in ministry, you'll do well never to show up in your p.j.'s (professional jealousy), which will always tear down meaningful associations.

Another formative process is discipline of study and further training. It is imperative that a shepherd feeds in order to effectively feed the flock. Christian educators lead the way, contributing to the disciplines of study. Their example inspires and motivates the shepherd to dig deeper, researching fresh material in a quest for wisdom and knowledge. Formal educational experience equips the minister with an arsenal of material, enabling him to feed and lead the flock.

It has been said that knowledge is power. Education is often the road to knowledge and can produce humility or pride depending on whether or not it goes to your head or heart. A great need exist for the shepherd to be one of the best-educated persons in the community. Equipped to expound the Word of God effectively and enabled to match wits and outthink the best minds the world possesses. One ought to know something about everything, if he can, but not to be presumed to be a know-it-all.

Education develops a worldview on how to relate to the executive in the high-rise office or to the down-and-out in hovels. No other person in the world needs more wisdom than he that comes in the name of the Lord. This person stands as God's ambassador, ready to speak instantly in or out of season. The first step is to ask God for wisdom, for rightly used knowledge is never exhausted, and all properly used wisdom and knowledge can be directed for the glory of God.

The journey for wisdom and knowledge is not so that one may boast about his sheepskins hanging on the wall, but that he has learned how to take knowledge gleaned and boil it down to simplistically defined principles with eternal values. A servant-leader specializes in timeless truths that will apply to all generations to come. Unless one can deliver the goods, degrees are useless. May God continue to give us educated, practical people for ministry, yet deliver us from educated fools.

Don't stop studying after formal training for that is only the beginning of your education. A professor encouraged me to commit to a life of study by his own example. He said with a yearning in his spirit to know more that with all his degrees and over three hundred hours of biblical language studies he had yet to scratch the surface in his quest for knowledge. I discovered then that my education formal and otherwise will be a never-ending journey full of wonderment and illumination. In the process of digesting spiritual input on a consistent, systematic routine, the shepherd is equipped for service.

Interpersonal relationship skills are imperative when working with the local church and its board. The pastor and church board are the local team leaders. Early believers elected a group of leaders from among themselves to participate in the daily ministration by serving tables. Providing for the church's physical necessities through food collected for distribution was a primary task. The administration of material necessities remains a present-day duty, as is the administration of fiscal matters. Though the pastor is the chief officer of the board, he should not be expected to carry the responsibility regarding these matters. Oversight from his team members keeps the shepherd well informed regarding the church's situation, enabling him to clearly know its pulse.

It serves the church well to provide gifts for the shepherd in the form of deacons to assume primary responsibilities for the church's fiscal and material matters. This ought to free the pastor to supervise with an unobstructed overview of ministries without being burdened down by daily incidentals. On occasions, boards may err in one of two ways: they are overcome with a new-founded self-importance and begin to exceed their prerogatives or they fail to live up to the responsibilities given to them. Another word of caution for team leaders: deacons or elders must refrain from a board-driven, heavy-handedly governance. Likewise, the pastor ought to refrain from dictatorially leading. Both are detrimental to the welfare of the church.

It is good for all these leaders to prayerfully revisit the doctrinal truth pertaining to their responsibilities and service. To be a deacon is to serve or to minister as a gift provided by God, being endowed and equipped for the work that is theirs to carry out. In most cases, spiritual influence and scriptural insight bringing these servant-leaders back to their original intent for serving the Lord, making them the efficient, helpful colleagues they are intended to be.

The appropriate relationship between deacons and pastors can be summed up in two words: the first is *cooperation*, with the implications of confidence, companionship, respect, obedience, and team building. The working together of cohorts with the kingdom of God as priority is a true pleasure in life. Pastors should not allow bad board encounters to turn them against healthy pastor-board relationships.

The second word is *trust*. I had just received a new charge with a hundred percent endorsement from the church after I went through an embattled situation. To say I was gun-shy of trusting another board is an understatement. Although my new cohorts outwardly displayed support, I knew a lot of work lay ahead to get them fully onboard with my vision.

A few months went by when the secretary, the main influencer, opened up speaking his heart at a board meeting. He began by recognizing my work ethic and dedication. Then he said, "Pastor, when you came I voted for you only because I knew you'd get it. However, today I want you and this board to know that I support and trust you completely and you're the boss." This person never once let me down even when we didn't agree. I had received newfound confidence and knew that I could trust my cohorts once again. Though I am not at that charge anymore, I know I have a true personal friend in that person who taught me to take the risk and trust again. There are people of God who will support God's chosen leader as long as that person strives to do right with a right spirit.

The executive board's responsibility for the community of faith is placed upon each member's shoulders, requiring personal relationships to be established. The essence of working together effectively as a board rests on seeing and understanding each other's points of view and in being flexible—not insisting on being right yet doing what is right. Leading and serving a church board requires intelligent organization and spiritual insight that will effectively move the church forward.

A heightened sensitivity for the shepherd's family is placed with paramount importance regarding his personal growth. This person needs to be spiritually constant and consistent in every area of his life. What worth would it be if the shepherd gained the whole community, yet in the process lost his most valuable and prized gifts—a loving spouse and caring children?

The first family of a church undergoes scrutiny that other families would not normally endure, such as scrutiny of their conduct, styles of dress, business, and recreation, to mention only a few. The proverbial bar is often thought to be set through the pastor's home. Many look to the pastors as examples for their own households. Scripture says "In all things showing yourself a pattern of good works" (Titus 2:7). It is God's will that a pastor and spouse set up their household to serve as a pattern.

The first lady of the parsonage ought to live with assurance that her spouse loves and respects her and their privacy. In an interview, as a young ordination candidate, the question was posed to me: who would come first in my life when both had prevalent pressing issues, the church or my spouse? I simply replied, "The Lord has blessed me with my wife, a lifelong companion, and she trumps everything else." We've always strived to maintain a special time strictly devoted for each other that is often very simple rather than elaborate. The key is to connect and communicate. For strong and renewed relationships to thrive, an initial and continual personal investment is required.

The spouse is quickly acknowledged as the most valuable player of a pastor's team. There are many varied ways that the spouse can be an indispensable participant in the pastoral work. She brings a proper safeguard and balance, connecting the roles of consultant and advisor, which can make or break the pastor. The intimate relationship between husband and wife gives her the insider knowledge about which buttons will set him off or render peace to his soul. She can shield him from his weaknesses or attack them according to her choice.

This co-laborer has been given great opportunity and responsibility in sharing in the pastorate. She partakes in moments of despondency and trials, knowing the struggles of her companion's mind and heart. This person possesses the power to give comfort, encouragement, and help, enabling the pastor to overcome his adversities. She is a good listener and confidante, as God is the silent listener to every conversation. The spouse is a burden-bearer and prayer warrior who remains faithful while paying the full price of self-sacrifice in order to partake of the rugged pathway with Christ and her companion pastor.

If the minister's relationship with his or her spouse is healthy, the more adept he or she will be ministering to the flock. A personal friend and mentor shared his proven formula for healthy marriage relationships, or as he calls it the five Ts of marriage. The first is thoughtfulness, due to how important it is for the companion to always know he or she is in the pastor's heart. It requires a caring conscientious consideration. Thoughtfulness clearly seeks to understand what the other is experiencing, feeling, and needing while expressing true love and concern. It underscores the fact that the other person is not taken for granted or forgotten, that he or she is clearly on your radar.

When you learn to practice thoughtfulness, the second T naturally follows—developing the habit of thankfulness. Thankfulness expresses kind recognition of another's actions, reciprocating the spirit in which they were initiated. The thankful heart will always express appreciation. We should be encouraged to be thankful for each other and for the simple deeds that are carried out to major acts of kindness.

The third T is talking, especially when it comes to the difficult topics. Listening is the key to communication. Most of us are not good listeners, yet we all like to talk. Think of it this way: none of us urge our newborn babies to listen, but we teach them to talk. We get them talking to the point that they seem to never stop without teaching them listening skills, which are vital to good communication. Hearing is effortless but listening regards effort.

It is well to pause and ask ourselves the following questions. Do I listen with my heart as well as my ears? Do I interrupt while the other person is speaking? Do I try to figure out what a person may say or am I listening? Do I make eye contact regularly? Am I careful with nonverbal messages? Do I repeat the essence of what has been said to ensure understanding? These are questions that will assist us in learning the skill of listening, which enhances our communication.

The fourth T is time. The pastor should aggressively set aside time for the nurturing of his or her household that often lives in a bubble for all to view. Time is a resource that we all have but often waste. Our time should be spent together engaging in meaningful activities. One's schedule should not be so busy that it doesn't allow for time for the most important people in your life. When you give someone the time of day, you're giving a part of yourself. It is natural to put off unwanted tasks as long as we can. It is also natural to choose those things we want to do first, just like eating dessert first thereby spoiling an appetite for the meal. This is a good place to initiate a time-management plan with emphasis on setting proper priorities. Always strive to ensure that your spouse and family get first dibs on your quality time.

The fifth T is tenderness. The quality of tenderness we have with each other will be dramatically influenced by the quality with which we practice thoughtfulness, thankfulness, talk, and time. Always remember to be kind and tenderhearted toward one another. Tenderness must not be linked with weakness. Jesus was tough as nails when the time came to laying His life down to become our sacrifice. However, Christ was kindhearted and gentle, desiring the meek, lowly, and little ones to approach Him. He is tough yet completely tender, having been likened to steel wrapped in velvet. Strive not to allow roughness to overshadow the tenderness within. Tenderness provides openness so others may enter your world. We certainly want our loved ones to know and experience the tenderness in our hearts we have towards them.

A healthy relationship with the children of the home contributes immensely to successful service. The minister's presence in the home breeds love, security, assurance, comfort, and confidence, providing fertile soil for young lives to grow. Children demand time for play and just plain fun, which helps alleviate some undue stress that is often incurred through service. The rough times seem to diminish when family becomes a priority. Thank God for children with the love and joy they inspire in families. The saying that the family that pray together stays together holds true if prayer is practiced regularly in the home.

Due to the nature of spiritual leadership, it is vital that prayer be given prominence for daily practice and continued growth. It has been said that a spiritual leader is as great publicly as he or she is on his or her knees before God privately. Without prayer one will do little good in the service of the Lord and need not expect much success unless he or she begins praying. The rejection of prayer ignores opportunities to meet God's presence. God has an open-door policy for us to approach Him in prayer believing He will grant whatever we need.

Prayer is nothing less than simple conversing with God. Striking up a dialogue with Him brings deep satisfaction and contentment. Why not? He is our Creator, and we are designed with the purpose of communing with Him. Talking to the God who made the universe and having His rapt attention *is* a big deal. It is more than a boring, mundane routine or dull ritual.

Sparks began to fly when Elijah prayed. The Earth began to quiver like a bowl of jelly when Paul prayed. The sun stood still and took notice in the heavens above when Joshua prayed. *Demons* trembled when Jesus prayed. Prayer recognizes the existence of a power that exceeds our own. Prayer helps to bring solutions to life's problems and protection and assurance that God is with us no matter how bad things are. God encourages us to call upon Him ("Call unto me, and I will answer thee, and shew thee great and mighty things, which thou knowest not." (Jeremiah 33:3)

I agree with the schoolboy who confessed to one of his school mates, "It may be unconstitutional, but I always pray before an exam." He understood that when the outlook was bad that nothing could keep him from looking up. Prayer focuses on the provider not the problem and assumes that the provider is bigger than the problem. Therefore, prayer bellies up to any challenge, believes that all things are possible with God, and boots out any thoughts of negativity. Our High Priest said, "Therefore, I say unto you, what things so ever you desire" (Mark 11:24).

God simply requests that we ask of Him. The great benefit of prayer is discovering when difficult circumstances occur that nothing is more valuable than a life connected to God in prayer. Your need may be weakness, so we pray for God's strength; our failures might beset us but we pray for forgiveness for having come short of the high calling in Christ. One's loneliness at the time of leadership can compel one to seek His presence by celebrating in prayer His love toward us. Through prayer we can trade our ignorance for God's insightfulness, our problems for His wisdom, and His healing for our sicknesses. God can do anything ("With men this is impossible; but with God all things are possible" (Matthew 19:26).

Jesus gave us the model prayer guide in Matthew 6:9-10. "Our Father which art in heaven, hallowed be thy name. Thy kingdom come Thy will be done in earth, as it is in heaven." When we pray, we should know that God is, and out of Him all things exist. The Lord's Prayer exemplifies our approach to prayer as one of respect, acknowledging and honoring His sovereign rule. Learn to pray for His will for every circumstance with assurance that He knows best and can guide our hearts. A heart of gratitude develops the right attitude in giving thanks to God for all things. "Give us this day our daily bread" (Matthew 6:11). Thanking the Lord for our daily sustenance recognizes His ability to provide His providential care on our behalf.

"And forgive us our debts, as we forgive our debtors" (Matthew 6:12). It is well to keep a clear conscience and clean heart by asking the Lord's forgiveness of all our wrongdoings and seeking His help in doing the right thing. When we forgive others, obstructions are torn down that destroy relationships and hinder God from answering prayers. Mt. 6:13a "And lead us not into temptation, but deliver us from evil" (Matthew 6:13). A good practice in prayer is seeking God's favor and strength to fight off temptation and deliver us from the evildoers' attacks which hinder us in doing God's will. Satan works feverously to interfere by doing all he can to deter people from praying, thereby rendering them ineffective on the battlefield of prayer. "For thine is the kingdom, and the power, and the glory, forever. Amen." (Matthew 6:13). At the close of the Lord's Prayer, we are reminded that God in glory is in control, and our sufficiency is found in Him.

Prayer brings one to a place of truth by forcing one to take inventory of self, allowing our hearts to mirror their secrets with the Holy Spirit's convictions. Truth will prevail in prayer and encourage one to be true to himself and God. Prayer leads to a position of submission. Hearts become pliable and easily directed. Submission in prayer is agreement in the revealed will of God flowing from a heart of obedience and leading us to pray with the right desires. Personal faith and conviction in which we expect God to meet with us in prayer is the right spirit that sets things in motion when we pray.

It is right to pray while putting your faith to work. Praying and believing are the dynamic duo that breaks through the chains of the impossible, perceives the invisible, laughs in the face of the insurmountable, fights inertia, and exalts the incomparable. Praying in faith is a strong expression of innermost assurance in God about what He knows and reveals as truth. If the desire is strong, benevolent, and not contrary to the providence of God, we can be assured that our prayers will be answered.

FAIR LEADERSHIP

PASTORS ARE SET APART WITH an anointing by the Holy Spirit, appointed and ordained to oversee the flock of God. They are to hold true to sound doctrine, guarding the sacred message and preaching the Word. Pastors are to lead God's people with compassion in healing ministry through prayer and anointing the sick. They serve in administrative capacities leading the church in decision-making and vision casting contributing to the church's mission. It is morally and spiritually right for the church to follow the guidance of a healthy and effective fair leader.

The moment a Christian leader can rightly position him or herself in all humility and ask others to follow, he is doing precisely what God has called him to do, and with reassurance the flock can move forward. The Holy Spirit continues to anoint servant-leaders with practical guidance in the administration of fair leadership, however let's face it; administering fairness in the lead chair can be a struggle when personal emotions are in play. This is where one's true character and integrity are on display.

The pastor's practice of fairness often incurs a variety of duties to ensure the community's spiritual welfare, all of which hinge on a pure and just heart filled with love for those trusted in his or her care. If a pastor is overwhelmed by the long list of needs, it can be to wearisome trying to keep up with the tasks fairly. Unfortunately, many pastors lack the ability to say no to the excessive demands imposed by their flock or enable others to become their armor-bearers.

"Pastors suffer an enormous burden, and the Christian message of service suggests (to some) an unlimited availability to others for whatever they need—even mowing grass for others."[106] The wise pastor will realize his limitations as well as acknowledge his giftedness. The pastor who continues striving to do it all will eventually burn out and his primary task will never reach its potential and his calling will be unfulfilled. A good practice is to permit oneself the opportunity to excel in strong personal giftedness while being surrounded by others who will shore up one's existing weaknesses. Yes, it is all right to say no and allow others to say yes.

The practice of the pastor is to look after the flocks as under-shepherds of Christ by way of His example as the chief shepherd. Following His death, burial and resurrection and prior to the ascension, Jesus instructed the disciples (leaders) not to leave Jerusalem "but wait for the promise of the Father, which, *saith he*, ye have heard of me" Acts 1:4 (KJV). The disciples were to receive the fullness of the Spirit so they too might have the power to witness and to go forth in ministry with great power and authority. The faithful under-shepherd understands that effective service is dependent on how much a person is willing to model a close-knit relationship with the chief shepherd. The Lord wants His workers to be well-equipped for service going forward in His name. This pattern would set precedence for future leaders of the church.

The image of shepherding the flock evokes a caring guide, not a cruel ruler. All people need sound teaching on biblical absolutes to morally guide and protect them throughout life. The shepherd directs the flock to green pastures through his personal discoveries of diligent, prayerful studies of the Word, making it easier for his flock to understand, assimilate, and apply the eternal rich truths. "The contemporary pastor must maintain a delicate balance between spending enough time with

---

106 McKnight, 269.

the members of the congregation to know their needs and spending enough time in the Word and prayer to have the resources to meet those needs."[107]

This involvement will take many different forms as every member is different. You may find yourself fishing at four in the morning or taking a day's journey on a mule, being sore for weeks to come. Sitting at Starbucks with professionals or hanging out at NASCAR. Other occasions may call for golfing on the green or mowing the green with a crew at the church. Attending the ladies' quilting guild for a devotion or meeting at city hall with the town fathers may add pressure for one to be proficient in all things. Don't be alarmed. You're not expected to be an expert in these fields, but your presence is in demand.

I remember the first funeral I participated in as a pastor. The local Methodist minister officiated while I was asked to be a pallbearer. My first thought was to say no, yet I had prayed with this man as he received the Lord and was honored the family thought of me. After the funeral, the seasoned Methodist minister shared with me his observation. He said, "You've learned a great lesson in recognizing that ministry is not always from the pulpit palace of fame. The ministry of presence can be far greater without saying one word."

Nothing can substitute interaction and personal involvement within the life of a community. Face time is imperative. People need to know their shepherd is approachable and in touch with their world. The shepherd takes pleasure and personal fulfillment as each member of the fold succeeds and grows, reaching their potential. He becomes their biggest fan cheering them onward to their accomplishments.

As much as the nice placid scene of green pastures and healthy congregations delight church leaders, one can be assured of conflicts as long as we continue to dwell together striving to serve one another

---

107 Wayne Kraiss, "The Pastor as Shepherd." *The Pentecostal Pastor a Mandate for the 21st Century,* compiled and ed. Thomas E. Trask, Wayde I. Goodall, and Zenas J. Bicket, 203–212 (Springfield, Mo.: Gospel Publishing House, 2006), 205.

in our imperfect world. This fact is not all dismal for it ought to direct us in overcoming differences, unifying our efforts, and putting Christ first in each life. Everyone has stories to tell of conflicts they have weathered that tested their personal resolve, character, and integrity.

One such personal story left me with the lesson not to allow conflict to let one be kicked off one's own front porch. I found myself entrenched with a dysfunctional board made up of individuals who had previously been discharged from and asked to leave other churches prior to my acceptance of this new charge. After the short honeymoon, key power players began to withhold their tithes in order to starve and move us out.

Obviously this board lacked shared vision and the desire to labor together. I had lost all my benefits with a huge decrease in salary leaving very little choice as to where to live. My wife and I decided to move into small evangelist quarters, putting the bulk of our house wares in storage. I had refused to indulge some of this board's disorderly and unbiblical practices, thereby incurring a lot of mistreatment and misrepresentation from these few members. It is true that only a few rotten potatoes can stink up the whole bunch, or in this case a few heathen-like backslidden churchmen who had erred from sound doctrine.

There are those conflicts that put one in mind of the story about the ole boy who got caught up in a tree with an angry raccoon. Amid all the screaming and yelling, the boy cries out to his buddy below who has a shotgun to just shoot up among us 'cause one of us has to have relief. That's the way I felt, so I called for the district officials to assist in settling some kind of resolution to this overwhelming conflict. At this point I certainly needed some overdue relief.

A major complaint from the board was that I had ceased shaking people's hands prior to service, which displayed an unwelcoming presence. Honestly, I did stop greeting people before the services, confining myself to my office in prayer so as to keep my composure and not to be cornered by their petty issues. I was tired of walking out into the foyer with a bull's-eye on my back.

Fortunately, God will vindicate His own servants and will litigate on their behalf. At the meeting, one of the five board members spoke to the officials on my behalf. He said, "Sir, if you had an old dog that sat on your porch, wagging his tail to welcome you home, yet all you did was to kick that old dog off the porch, do you really think that dog would stay on the porch for long? No, sir. They've been kicking my pastor off his porch, and frankly, I am tired of their behavior along with other issues I have with them." To say the least, the officials, that deacon, and a majority of the congregation stood by their pastor, desiring my continued service as the conflict was resolved, resulting in a few departures from that board.

Sometimes the best resolution is to have a parting of the ways. We know Paul the apostle and Barnabas after having a disagreement departed to their own way. My dad always told me there would be times that I should not to go away mad or sad, but just go away and move onward to a new day. Be sure not to allow yourself to be kicked off your own front porch due to the misgivings and conflicts of a few. The church did rebound and began fruitful ministry once again in the community.

Nine years later, having moved back into the area, one of the men who opposed my ministry surprisingly met me at a local Wal-Mart. I was selecting a tricycle for my son's Christmas gift. He approached me saying, "Pastor Steve, it's good to see you," and proceeded telling me with penitence in his heart how he had lied and misrepresented me during our tenure. He was sorry that he was a part of those striving to run me out of town. He then humbly asked for my forgiveness.

I stated, "Sir, I was your shepherd then and I loved and forgave you of all wrongdoing, and nothing has changed from then to now." With relief sweeping over his countenance, he then confessed that not one day in the previous nine years did he go to bed without thinking or praying for my family's well-being. That day a lot of overdue healing took place with two brothers overcoming an old conflict.

A friend imparted some sound advice while I was engaged in another conflict with some local power brokers. Though I was well within my rights and very well could have brought legal action, it was not in my heart to do so. My friend said, "It is good to remember that no matter who is in the right, when you get in a fight with a skunk you both come out stinking, win or lose." The moral of his wisdom was that conflicts should be approached with a resolve to remain objective, joined with a deep sensitivity to fairness for all concerned. Strive always to give a back door for the opponent to have a graceful exit. It is better for that person to leave with the hope of future restoration regarding their relationship than to be scorned and never to be salvaged.

It serves one well to have a guide to serve as reference when engaging in conflicts. An effective conflict-management consists of the following steps: inquire to listen and understand the situation; identify the characteristics of the conflict, getting to the heart of the matter; strive to isolate the problem including those persons who have need to know; innovate a process of resolution tailored to the need and implement resolutions; and finally, invigilate the conflict or monitor the process of restoration and recovery by giving careful oversight to the process. Both church and personal conflicts can be resolved through scriptural principles of Christian conduct such as repentance, confession, forgiveness, humility, grace, and mercy for all sides of the issue.

The act of courageous leadership during perilous times and not renouncing Christ is itself a witness that Peter shares with the shepherds. Shepherds often defend the fold against dangerous adversaries encountering spiritual warfare. "He takes the initiative and battles the enemy of the members of his congregation. It is not because he is personally under attack or threatened. It is because those who have been entrusted to his care are threatened."[108]

A key concept to remember about conflicts is not to allow them to intimidate or threaten your insightful understanding and confidence in the situation. Rather, approach the matter with prayerful intrepidity, striving to make the right choice. At times one might ask, "Am I reaping more than what I've ever sowed?" When a shepherd encounters conflicts and adversities, he must never forget who called him to serve in the first place so he may remain true to his post.

---

108 Kraiss, 207.

RIGHT ATTITUDE

THE RIGHT ATTITUDE OF A pastor's role is grounded in servant leadership that is conducted with proper intent of personal willingness and a sense of divine calling, not a sense of internal or external coercion. A pastor's view of his role as an overseer needs to have a positive motivation to let him accomplish pastoral ministry. When the intent of service is properly grounded, the servant has a ready mind, a forward spirit, and a strong will to serve. A rule to remember is that attitude reflects leadership.

The shepherd's disposition will always precede his position among the flock. Followers will latch on to a leader's attitude faster than his or her actions. Our attitudes determine what we perceive through our circumstances and how we manage our feelings. The right attitude will set precedence for right responses as attitudes are the most influential assets a leader can possess. Positive and good attitudes are like a common cold, spreading to a pandemic if allowed to.

The right attitude will insist on getting over and working through problematic issues. Our personal struggle with attitude illustrates how the right disposition can be beneficial. With that in mind, my wife Tammy was terrified when the doctor sadly told her that she had Multiple Sclerosis, a cruel, dreadful, debilitating disease with no known absolute cure, was at work in her body.

Stunned with fright and dreading the unknown future, she gradually realized she was losing mobility in her legs. A crutch or walker became her traveling companion. It was something she could no longer hide. Femininity rebelled but to no avail, so she decided to hibernate. No one could see her struggles when she hid behind closed doors, and that became her small, shriveled-up world.

While visiting parishioners, I met our sons' doctor in the stairwell at the hospital, and after a brief greeting he inquired about Tammy's condition. I told him that she had basically locked herself in the house and didn't want to be seen in public. Knowing that his wife, a pediatrician and practicing partner in the children's clinic, also has MS, I expected to hear some high tech explanation and sobbing sympathy, but what a surprise I got instead. His advice was all about attitude.

The doctor very simply told me to tell Tammy to get over it and get on with life. I mustered the courage to deliver his message. It was a jolt, and it might have made us mad, but we took it in stride. She took the doctor's advice like a bitter dose of medicine, and today she is walking and carrying on a reasonably normal life. It all started with three jarring words: *Get over it.* How many "get over its" do we have in our attitude?

Don't allow setbacks to stop you. If at first you don't succeed, try, try, and try again. The *secret* of a successful over comer is to have and maintain faith with the right attitude. The wrong attitude can be detrimental as it may lead to further bad decisions and foster a low self esteem. Often when we face adversity we put up a wall that Superman couldn't leap over or tear down. It puts a snarl on our faces and not a smile. We get catty and not compassionate. But *get over it.* A bad attitude is not worth what it costs. When attitude does not align itself with its proper intent, this is the moment for an attitude check. Charles Swindoll has said,

> The longer I live, the more I realize the impact of attitude on life. Attitude, to me, is more important than facts. It is more important than the past, than education, than money, than circumstances, than failures, than successes, than what other people think or say or do. It is more important than appearance, giftedness, or skill. It will

make or break a company, a church, or a home. The remarkable thing is that we have a choice every day regarding the attitude we will embrace for that day. The only thing that we can do is play on the one string we have, and that is our attitude. I am convinced that life is 10 percent what happens to me and 90 percent how I react to it. We are in charge of our attitudes.[109]

Church leadership that is inappropriately motivated by wrong attitudes is not to be offered to God. The intent of begrudging service will never please God, only offend Him. C.S. Lewis stated, "Every time you make a choice you are turning the control part of you, the part that chooses, into something a little different from what is was before. And taking your life as a whole, with all your innumerable choices, you are slowly turning this control thing either into a heavenly creature or into a hellish one."[110] Serve for the right reasons. Ministry should not be an unwanted burden; pastors are not to serve out of a sense of false guilt or fear, or in an attempt to please people. Any of these attitudes or motives can lead to unwillingness to shepherd or a tendency to shepherd in an inappropriate manner.

The pastor of a flock is not to be motivated by greed for financial gain but have enthusiasm to serve others. The misconceptions of the ministry as a mere profession, a means of livelihood, a service to humanity, or possessing giftedness can be misleading and lead to attributing to the wrong reason for servant leadership. Excess of love for money brings selfish division between God and those who have interest at hand. Eventually a person who is possessed by the craving for excessive monetary gain inherits the alienation from God and others. The right attitude for a pastor is his eagerness to give and not the desire to take.

---

109 Chuck Swindoll, *Improving Your Serve* (Waco, Tex.: Word, 1981).
110 C.S. Lewis, *Mere Christianity* (New York: MacMillan, 1952), 86.

EXEMPLIFY THE MISSION OF GOD

FINALLY, THEY ARE TO SERVE "not by domineering ... but by being examples" I Peter 5:3. Jesus clearly pointed out that the way of the world at large was for leaders to domineer over the led, expecting obedience and the perks of leadership without resistance. Pastors who lead by domineering instead of example often are threatened by other gifted individuals and lack self-confidence. These people are not usually comfortable in their own skins and find leading a team awkward.

When they do not get their way in particular issues, they set out to complain. They then threaten to leave and begin to move in the direction that strengthens their cause using authority and position. A domineering leader may often refuse to delegate leadership responsibilities which clearly signify a lack of trust in God and one's own abilities. Efforts to lead by this model hinder the work of kingdom business due to its selfishly embedded intent for personal interest.

Pastors are not to lord over the people, meaning to behave in a high-handed, heady, or dictatorial way. Rather, they should be examples for others in the community to follow. Lording it over the people in a congregation is not the same as leading people in the congregation. The danger of lording it over other people is failing to show them proper respect.

"A good shepherd does not drive or herd the sheep from the rear of the flock. When driven, the flock may exhibit frustration and bewilderment.

The driven flock responds from fear of retaliation. They are required to go in a certain direction or suffer unpleasant consequences."[111] Shepherds are to lead with a mutual respect and trust reciprocated by the flock. The ancient shepherd did not drive his sheep, but walked in front of them and called them to follow.

The ancient example serves as a call to humbly assist others in genuine love and honor by showing preference for others and their needs. It is of necessity that leadership exemplifies the primal mission of the church through the life and teaching of the leader. The church's God-given mission consists of edification, worship, evangelism, and compassion. These are the vehicles necessary to fulfill the original purpose of the church's great commission given by Christ: "Go ye therefore, and teach all nations, baptizing them in the name of the Father, Son, and Holy Spirit: teaching them to observe all things whatsoever I have commanded you" (Matthew 28:19–20).

Edification

Leading the Example of Edification encourages spiritual fellowship to demonstrate observable love and care to one another as commanded by the Lord. "A new command I give you: Love one another. As I have loved you, so you must love one another" (John 13:34). "The individual does not disappear behind the vague contours of a 'totality,' but he is liberated from individualization and solitariness in order to have a place in this new fellowship."[112] The believer becomes an active participant in a loving family that develops relationships which glorify Christ.

Paul encouraged the edification of the body of Christ. "In Ephesians 4:12, for example, he indicates that God has given various gifts to the church 'to prepare God's people for works of service, so that the body of

---

111 Kraiss, 207.
112 William B. Berkouwer, *Studies in Dogmatics The Church* (Grand Rapids, Mich.: Eerdmans, 1976), 77.

Christ may be built up.' The potential for edification is the criterion by which all activities, including our speech, are to be measured."[113]

Educating the believer in godly doctrines builds him or her up by adding to his or her faith. "Consequently, faith comes from hearing the message, and the message is heard through the word of Christ" (Romans 10:17). Teaching all that Christ commanded nurtures and educates the believer to participate in the building up of the church. Further gifts of the Holy Spirit are bestowed to the church "the manifestation of the Spirit is given to every man to profit withal" (1 Corinthians 12:7 KJV).

These gifts are intended for the building up and sanctification of the church for the common good. The church's life and ministry includes the power of the Holy Spirit in demonstrated gifts of the Spirit that are manifest through a diversity of people and means. The challenges the body of Christ encounters meeting a multitude of needs should deepen our awareness and dependence on the Spirit's gifts to the church. The church cannot be complete without the Spirit's provisions.

"Every member of Christ's body has a special function and should contribute his or her gift(s) for its strengthening. Spiritual gifts should not cease to operate before the Lord's return (I Cor. 13:8–13)."[114] These gifts must work in cooperation with the Spirit and the believer as the Spirit distributes them accordingly to His will, they are characterized by grace (1 Corinthians 12:11). "Christians do not have to attain some level of holiness or spirituality in order to receive spiritual gifts. They are a reflection of God's grace to the church and made available to every believer."[115] Paul uses the word *charismata* meaning "gifts" in 1 Corinthians 12:4. The word *charis* (Gk.) or "grace" signifies spiritual gifts are primarily gifts of grace.

---

113 Erickson, 1063.
114 Craig S. Keener, *Gift & Giver* (Grand Rapids, Mich.: Baker Academic, 2001), 96.
115 William W. Menzies and Robert P. Menzies, *Spirit and Power* (Grand Rapids, Mich.: Zondervan, 2000), 180.

We need not rely solely on human instrumentation in response to the spiritual building up of the church or those in need of spiritual help. The purpose of spiritual gifts is to build up or edify the household of faith (1 Corinthians 14:26). These gifts are given for the common good with the goal of edifying the body of the church (1 Corinthians 12:7). They must be used not in pride or for personal exaltation, but with sincere desire to help others and with a heart which genuinely cares for others. "J. I. Packer says that our exercise of spiritual gifts is nothing more or less than Christ himself ministering through his body to his body, to the Father, and to all mankind. Christ from heaven uses Christians as his mouth, his hand, his feet, even his smile."[116]

The gifts are not listed in any particular order in the Bible, nor does the Bible mention a difference between obviously supernatural and apparently less supernatural gifts. They flow from the Spirit's work interrelated and involving a variety of manifestations. "God touches all our abilities and potential with supernatural power. All Spirit-imparted abilities to minister and meet the needs of the church are derived from the enabling of the gift of the Spirit."[117]

To categorize these gifts for convenience, they are gifts of leadership, power, revelation, and utterance. The ministry leadership gifts to the church (Ephesians 4:11) speak of apostles, prophets, evangelists, pastors, teachers. "The role of leadership is not control, but peace. Leadership, rightfully used, should create confidence in people to discover and use the gifts God has given them and to understand their purpose — that is, the intent of the Spirit — the edifying and building up of the church (I Cor. 14:12)."[118]

---

116 Anthony D. Palma, *Holy Spirit a Pentecostal Perspective* (Springfield, Mo.: Gospel Publishing House, 2001), 193.
117 David Lim, *Spiritual Gifts: A Fresh Look* (Springfield, Mo.: Gospel Publishing House, 2003), 45.
118 J. Lowell Harrup, "The Ministry and Gifts of the Holy Spirit Today: Cooperating with the Spirit," *Enrichment 10*, no.1 (Winter 2005), 105.

Apostle is linked with *shaliach*, a Jewish term meaning "sent one" as commissioned by the authorities. In a restricted sense, apostle refers to the original leaders of the church and is unrepeatable. Many believers today view New Testament apostles as missionaries who continued to serve in fulfilling a specific call. "There is a continuation of apostolic ministry indicated through the Holy Spirit (Acts 5:32). Stanley M. Horton observes apostolic ministry … is a church-building, fellowship-building work, exercised with accompanying miracles that are the work of the Spirit."[119] Apostolic ministry is the role of spiritual leadership that includes godly maturity, scriptural experience, integrity, and compassionate works all wrapped in humility.

> H. Maurice Lednicky has identified seven primary characteristics of apostolic ministry today (1) Anointed and uncompromising proclamation of the gospel; (2) Authentic, Christ-exalting miracles and manifestations; (3) Establishing and reproducing viable New Testament churches; (4) Spiritual mentors who scripturally train developing leaders; (5) Protect and preserve Scriptural truth; (6) Define and defend Biblical holiness; and (7) Understand and practice servant leadership.[120]

Prophets were those in the church who spoke under the direct impulse of the Holy Spirit, whose main motivation and concern was with the spiritual life and purity of the church. "The term prophet applied in general to anyone who spoke for God. In the broadest sense it could apply to all witnessing Christians. In Ephesians, Paul often couples prophets with apostles as contemporary expositors of God's mysteries bound in the Bible (2:20; 3:5)."[121] Prophets were known to provide divine direction for the church, illuminating God's directives so the people

---

119 Palma, 209.
120 James K. Bridges, *Pentecostal Gifts & Ministries in a Postmodern Era* (Springfield, Mo.: Gospel Publishing House, 2004), 145.
121 Keener, 131.

of God could influence one another in the wisest way. Many prophets brought insightful practical truths that had already been received, as in the case of Silas and Judas bringing the decision of the Jerusalem Council to Antioch.

The ministry of a prophet does not need a title or position, only a brokenness and intent desire to stand in the gap pleading for God to forgive us instead of for God to give us. In the article "Apostles and Prophets," the General Presbytery reached seven basic conclusions identifying and relating to prophetic ministry during the New Testament period. These conclusions are

> (1) there were recognized groups of prophets in the early churches often closely associated with the apostles; (2) the apostles themselves (as Barnabas, Silas [both of whom on occasion appear to be recognized as apostles], Saul [Paul], and John) also functioned as prophets (Acts 13:1; 15:32; Rev. 1:3); (3) these prophets did travel on occasion from church to church; (4) both men and women were recognized as prophets; (5) although never appointed to ruling functions in their capacity as prophets (as were overseers/elders), prophets did exercise spiritual influence with the apostles and elders in the belief and practice of the Early Church; (6) the integrity of the prophet was maintained by authentic inspired utterance that was true to the Scriptures and apostolic doctrine; and (7) there is no provision for qualifying or appointing prophets as a part of a church leadership hierarchy for succeeding generations."[122]

The evangelist's ministry was different than that of a prophet. "The evangelist did not go to churches. He went where the sinners were. Prophets went to the churches. In a sense, the prophets were revival men."[123] The evangelist's work is to proclaim the gospel to non-Christians, gaining converts as God desires. Jesus gave the supreme example of an

---

122 Bridges, 156.
123 Stanley M. Horton, *What the Bible Says about the Holy Spirit* (Springfield, Mo.: Gospel Publishing House, 2005), 269.

evangelist coming "not to condemn the world but to save the world through Him" (John 3:17).

"Evangelists served the church by announcing the word that brought people into the church to begin with. They were frontline warriors, because the one piece of armor specifically designed for advancing into enemy territory and the one offensive weapon are both related to the gospel (Eph. 6:15, 17)."[124] Evangelists mobilized and convinced others in the local congregation to join with them in reaching out to others to build up the body of Christ.

Obviously, the ministry gift of pastors has been greatly illustrated, yet Scripture is clear these are true gifts from Christ to His church. Pastors are diligent watching over souls placed in their charge, knowing there will come a time of personal accountability. This gift cannot be manufactured by means of a special discipline of training. It is God who causes people to oversee His body, setting up governments within the church (1 Corinthians 12:28–30). A pastor will possess a heart consumed with love for the people of God and a heart on fire for God.

Teachers have a God-given gift to talk about and make known God's Word in order to build up the community of faith in the Holy Spirit. "The word 'teacher' in Eph. 4:11 and throughout most of the New Testament is derived from the Greek word *didaskalos*, meaning "one who is able to instruct."[125] The teaching gift established a separate leadership group, even though the function of teaching was also given to the pastor. Pastor and former bible college president Wayne Benson says, "While it is possible to teach without pastoring, it is not possible to pastor without teaching."[126] Teachers could have been itinerant within the churches, not having to stay in one location as pastors did. Acts 18:27 endorses Apollos as a teacher on the move having "helped them much", meaning the people in various churches where he ministered.

---

124 Keener, 131.
125 Bridges, 194.
126 Ibid., 193.

The teacher adds to the edification of the body of Christ as he breaks the bread of life, bringing eternal truths and imparting the wisdom of God to believers.

Teachers did not cause division unless it was unavoidable where false teaching in the community existed. Their goal was to build up the body and not divide it. They would bring insightful answers in response to confusing and troubling issues. Teachers are on the same page as pastors in promoting unity and the purpose of the church's mission. Teaching the truth is essential in order to expose the false doctrines that creep their way into the mind and spirit of a people and lead to conflict.

Sound instruction enables stability, consistency and maturity to be fostered and formed in the body of Christ. Donald Gee says:

> The real teacher who is a gift from Christ will usually be orderly in his discourses, for that is of the very essence of his own particular ministry; quite consistently he may speak from notes and follow a carefully prepared sequence of thought; but at the heart of it all is a supernatural gift of the Spirit quite distinct from the same outward process followed by a teacher leaning only to the natural mind and limited strictly to natural resources.[127]

Teachers are dedicated to study the Word of God, clothed in humility, possessing faith, and expecting God to teach them more allowing the Holy Spirit to use their giftedness to bless the body.

Pentecostal empowerment of the church became a normative experience for Christians allowing the gifts of the Spirit to operate freely and on the spur of the moment as needed. "To act spontaneously means to respond to the impulses or promptings of the Holy Spirit to do or say things we did not plan to do or say at that moment. The gifts of the Spirit described in I Cor. 12:4–11 and 14:26 are ways the Spirit may manifest

---

127 Bridges, 198.

himself spontaneously."[128] The gifts of power are faith, healings, and working of miracles.

The gift of faith (1 Corinthians 12:9) is a divine assurance that God will cause the supernatural to invade the natural for specific needs. Faith is supernatural confidence and belief that God can perform the miraculous. "The gift of faith is a miraculous faith for a special situation or opportunity. It is not saving faith or faithfulness that develops as a fruit of the Spirit. The vibrant, active Christian is more likely to see this gift in action as he claims God's power for present needs."[129] This faith is imparted by the Holy Spirit enabling belief in the extraordinary and miraculous.

God gives all Christians faith in order to accomplish their giftedness in the body of Christ (Romans 12:3, 6). The goal of faith is not to receive what we want, but to accomplish God's assignment. "Nothing God calls us to accomplish is impossible if Christians exercise complete faith. 'Moving mountains' was a Jewish figure of speech for doing what was virtually impossible, and Jesus had promised that nothing would be impossible to those who exercised even the smallest amount of faith (Mark 11:34)."[130]

The gift of healing (I Cor. 12:9) is given to restore physical health by divinely supernatural means drawing attention to the gospel of Jesus Christ. Stanley M. Horton emphasizes that the gift can be exercised only at the prompting of the Spirit when he says there is 'no evidence that the apostles were able to heal whenever they felt like it by some resident power of healing'. The gift is given to a person for the healing of another person.[131] It is because of God's faithfulness to Jesus' name (Acts 3:12) that He heals, not with respect to any power or piety on our behalf. Jesus has

---

128 Roger D. Cotton, "Walking in the Spirit in Spontaneity," *Paraclete* 25, no. 1 (Winter 1991): 1–2.
129 Lim, 75.
130 Keener, 117.
131 Palma, 220.

not changed His willingness to heal those who will come to Him, nor has His power declined.

> While we should trust that God will often (or even normally) answer prayers for healing and should follow our Lord's example of compassion toward the physically as well as emotionally and spiritually wounded, we should also avoid assuming that anyone who is not healed is spiritually deficient. God does not always heal right away, and sometimes, for whatever reason, God does not heal in this life.[132]

The working of miracles (1 Corinthians 12:10) is another way the gift of faith is manifested. "Miracles are a translation of the Greek word *dunamis*, which is often translated 'power' and is a comprehensive term for wonder-inducing works of all kinds."[133] Literally, miracles mean demonstrations of power, a definition implying that many kinds of miracles overlap the gifts of faith and healing. Miracles occur by God's command (1 Kings 18:36) as He keeps the universe by His might and regularly performs miracles without human intervention (Exodus 3:2; John 5:17, 21).

He often delights to perform various miracles through His servants at the request of someone close to Him (2 Kings 1:10) for the church's edification and bringing glory to His name.

> Acting on a word from the Lord is not the same thing as 'confessing' or 'claiming' that something should happen, as if we ourselves, rather than God, have authority to speak things into being (Lam. 3:37; Rom. 4:17). We should also recognize that for the edification of the body of Christ, gifts related to God's Word are ranked higher than this spectacular gift (I Cor. 12:28), though at the same time, miracles are extraordinarily effective in securing people's attention for evangelism. (Acts 14:3)[134]

---

132 Keener, 118.
133 Palma, 221.
134 Keener, 119.

Miracles are not an explanation of normal events, a postponement, or an intermission of nature, yet they may interrupt the natural order as we know it. "God's realm is beyond human comprehension. He does not have to change His procedures or laws in order to help us. Miracles may have to do with providing protection, giving provision, casting out demons, altering circumstances, or passing judgment."[135]

The gifts of revelation are word of wisdom, knowledge, and discerning of spirits (I Cor. 12:8, 10). "The gift of wisdom, rather than prophecy is the gift for guidance. It is not a bestowal of wisdom but a message of wisdom and those ministering this message are not necessarily wiser than others."[136] A word of wisdom is a declaration of a wise utterance spoken and enabled by the Holy Spirit to meet particular needs with practical application of the Word and can be understood as speaking wisely.

> In a manifestation of the spiritual gift of the word of wisdom something flashes. There is a sense of the divine, a consciousness of an utterance transcending all the garnered stores of merely human experience. One is deeply conscious that the supremely right thing has been said and the true course of action indicated. No further appeal is desired because the heart rests in a calm satisfaction that the will of God has been revealed.[137]

We should make the mission of God's wisdom our principal priority (Proverbs 4:7). "The fear of the Lord is the beginning of wisdom" (Proverbs 9:10). The word of wisdom can represent the revealing of divine mysteries founded on God's truths and purposes rather than human understanding.

The word of knowledge "and the knowledge of the holy is understanding," (Proverbs 9:10) bringing deeper insight of the Scripture

---

135 Lim, 78.
136 Ibid., 71.
137 Donald Gee, *Concerning Spiritual Gifts* (Springfield, Mo.: Gospel Publishing House, 1972), 32–33.

inspired by the Holy Spirit revealing "supernatural illumination that has to do with the knowledge of God, Christ, the gospel, and the applications to Christian living."[138] This gift could be revealed in a more supernatural way. All knowledge is with the Lord, and it is not unreasonable to believe that the Holy Spirit would impart a manifestation of this divine knowledge at any given moment as He wills.

The source of all manifestations of the Spirit is God who knows all things. A revelation coming out of the omniscience of the Almighty can be justly called a word of knowledge. "Sometimes God reveals to a person someone's sin or special need or His own activity on someone's behalf. These are facts only God can know."[139]

Discerning of spirits (1 Corinthians 14:29) applies to making a distinction between spirits whether human, demonic, or the Holy Spirit. "Primarily, the gift of discernment of spirits is the Spirit-conferred capacity to judge the origin and content of prophecy. It is legitimate to apply this terminology to the gift of discerning the origin and content of any spiritual manifestation."[140] Discerning of spirits involves forming a judgment with supernatural perception, discerning that which is good or evil, true or false, and decision-making. This gift assists in judging prophecies to distinguish whether an utterance is from the Holy Spirit or not and guards the church against false prophets and teachers.

The gifts of utterance include speaking in tongues, interpretation, and prophecy. Tongues are languages directed by the Holy Spirit bringing anointing and edification. The gift of tongues is the same in essence as speaking in tongues, but different in purpose and use (1 Corinthians 12:4–10, 28). In corporate worship, tongues are brought forth by the same unction followed by an interpretation (1 Corinthians 14:4). Tongues are

---

138 Horton, 272–273.
139 Lim, 73.
140 International Dictionary of Pentecostal Charismatic Movements, s.v. "Discernment of Spirits-Terminology."

given for the edification of the body and as a sign so that unbelievers may attest to the Spirit's manifestation and believe.

The interpretation gift is given to the one speaking in tongues or someone else (1 Corinthians 14:13). The essential meaning of interpretation is translation where the translator makes sense out of the unknown tongue by the Spirit's enabling revelation. "The gift may come in a variety of ways, 'either by vision, by burden, or by suggestion, just as the Lord may choose'. A step of faith may be required also in that the Spirit very often gives only a few words of the interpretation at first. Then, when these are given in faith, the rest comes as the Spirit gives the interpretation."[141]

These two gifts operate in harmony to insure order and edification of the body. "As the source of prophetic inspiration, the Spirit grants special revelation and inspired speech. These twin functions are exemplified by the many instances where the rabbis speak of 'seeing' or 'speaking in the Spirit'."[142] The interpretation makes known the meaning of an utterance given in tongues that all may understand and be edified by. "Tongues served as evidence that Jesus gave the Spirit to inspire the apostles to speak of the crucified, risen, and exalted Lord, had received this authority from the Father. When Spirit filled believers speak in tongues, they witness that Jesus rules as Savior"[143]

Prophecy serves to build up the congregation (1 Corinthians 14:4) for strengthening, comfort, and encouragement. "Prophecy is a supernatural communication designed primarily to help believers in their Christian walk. Prophesying means translating the Christian faith into the very situation of the hearer..."[144] This gift enables a believer to bring a word

---

141 Horton, 279.

142 Robert P. Menzies, "Coming to Terms With an Evangelical Heritage—Part 2: Pentecostals and Evidential Tongues." *Paraclete*, 28/4 (Fall 1994), 5.

143 Benny C. Aker and Edgar R. Lee, "Naturally Supernatural: The Baptism of the Spirit," *Signs & Wonders in Ministry Today,* ed. Benny C. Aker & Gary B. McGee (Springfield, Mo.: Gospel Publishing House, 1996), 91.

144 Palma, 211.

from God under the Holy Spirit's guidance. These words should be tested as to their genuineness and conformity to the truth.

Prophecy reveals the secrets of hearts and can include any message received from the Lord. God has spoken to His people through prophecy from the very beginning in diverse ways: through visions, dreams, audible voices, ecstatic trances, and through the Spirit inspiring words in the heart of the prophet. Theologian David Lim states that "Paul is referring to the giving of Spirit-inspired, spontaneous messages, not the preaching of sermons. A basic relationship between revelation and prophecy exists: the Spirit illumes us to see the unfolding progress of the kingdom of God; the secrets of a person's heart are revealed; the sinner is put under conviction (I Cor. 14:24–25)."[145]

There are other gifts of the Spirit that are practical in nature and resident in the life of believers (Romans 12:6–8) including serving, giving, showing mercy, helps, exhortation, and administration that assist the community of faith. The gift of service or ministry in Romans 12:7 refers to the work of a deacon yet it is not limited to deacons. The Spirit enables those in His service to fulfill their respective office with wisdom and power to ensure that they have the spiritual capacity to practically serve the body. Romans 12:8 discusses those who give have a divine preference to give of personal possessions and yet giving in abundance beyond their own wealth. They possess a liberal and generous spirit, sharing without an underlying motive for self and with no strings attached.

People who show mercy are those who can easily sympathize and emphasize with another, enabling them to cheerfully assist the sick, poor, aged, disabled, and prisoner. Helps means ministering to the weak (Acts 20:35) and showing kindness (1 Timothy 6:2). Exhortation carries the idea of conciliating, which is included with the gift of prophecy (1 Corinthians 14:3). Administration (governments) refers to managing

---

145 Lim, 79.

practical business of the church as well as spiritual leadership and is not limited to elected officials (1 Corinthians 12:28).

The church must not assume that these are the only gifts God gives, for as many needs that are present in the body so are gifts provided to minister to them. "The very diversity of the gifts Paul mentions summons us to be open to more of God's work than just the way he has worked among us in the past. We should not play down the significance of any gift God has for us, it is easy to focus so much on one gift that we are unaware of entire areas of spiritual experience."[146] Through the diversity and administration of all the spiritual gifts, some vulnerability of misuse could easily spoil the divine gift to fail in its divine purpose.

The church at Thessalonica erred in suppressing spiritual gifts of utterances, and Paul encouraged them not to quench the Spirit or despise prophesying (1 Thessalonians 5:19–21). The Pentecostal scholar Donald Gee provides two principles that would cure practically every abuse of the gifts of the Spirit. "There is a golden rule governing the right exercise of spiritual gifts; it is found in I Cor. 14:26 *Let all things be done unto edifying*. And there is a golden principle which alone can make them really profitable, the principle of love—enunciated so explicitly in I Cor. 13 written especially in connection with spiritual gifts."[147] The importance and use of spiritual gifts ought to reflect three provisions: do they exalt Jesus Christ, do they edify the church, and are they governed by the greatest of all gifts, which is love.

Worship

Leading an example of worship attributes glory and honor to our sovereign Lord, fulfilling our innate desire in manifesting spiritual praise and adoration. "A. W. Tozer once wrote that worship is 'the missing jewel of the church.' His description of worship as a jewel is appropriate. Of

---

146 Keener, 134–135.
147 Donald Gee, *After Pentecost* (Springfield, MO: Gospel Publishing House, 1945), 88.

all the things a church does, none is more precious and beautiful than worship."[148] The mission of the church centers praise and exaltation to God. The attention is for the people of God to recognize and declare His greatness while connecting with Him in an active process. This places God as the priority of worship rather than one's self-centered satisfaction with his or her own way of thinking. "We worship for one reason only, because God is God and He is worthy of our adoration. Anything less is manipulative and selfish and cancels real worship by substituting humanism disguised in religious trappings."[149]

People desire to experience God when they worship. Connecting with our Creator is intuitive, as the need is woven into the fabric of our being. How worship manifests itself comes in many ways. For example, when a colleague of mine gave an altar call, an old man came forward for prayer. Other men gathered around to pray, and something unexpected to happen. In the excitement while he prayed, his overalls came unsnapped and fell to his feet. While the men around him assisted him, it appeared to the congregation they were getting spiritually blessed. The pastor's wife observed the commotion around the altar from her place at the piano and discerned the Spirit was moving, not knowing the man had lost his trousers. She began to play more fervently, and with others in the congregation following her lead the church erupted into dynamic worship. Though the man suffered a twinge of embarrassment through it all, the church left with their own unique God encounter.

The author of Hebrews encourages believers not to give up meeting together as some made a habit of missing church (Hebrews 10:25). The phrase "not give up meeting together" implies desertion, abandonment, and lack of commitment to the assembly. It is important for the spiritual health and welfare of believers to attend church regularly focusing on God, instruction from the Word, and fellowship with one another.

---

148 William J. Martin, *The Church in Mission* (Springfield, Mo.: Gospel Publishing House, 1996), 82.

149 Martin, 86.

True worship is engaged on the spirit's level, which is in keeping with God's nature. "God is spirit, and his worshipers must worship in spirit and in truth" (John 4:24). "The key to effective worship in the healthiest settings is engaging people's hearts, minds, souls, and strength. To be engaged in worship involves varying styles and forms, but is focused on actively drawing in and involving God's people."[150]

The church is privileged to worship the Lord, clapping and cheering the great God it serves and loves. The psalmist says in 44:8, "In God we make our boast all day long, and we will praise your name forever." Psalm 150 includes every believer in the biblical command, "Let everything that has breath praise the Lord." Again the psalmist said, "Praise the Lord, O my soul; all my inmost being, praise his holy name. Praise the Lord, O my soul, and forget not all is benefits " (Psalm 103:1–2). The excitement of worship rises and reaches a new crescendo as we are encouraged in Psalm 47:1 to "[c]lap your hands, all you nations; shout to God with cries of joy." The early church came together to praise God and be edified. Thereafter, they went forth to reach out to the lost, and the Lord added to their number (Acts 2:46–47).

There are times when the method of doing worship can destroy its original intent. God's love is certainly put to the test, yet is proved time and again. It is well for us to discover how far this love will take us while dealing with practical issues of worship and leadership. At a church growth meeting, the topic of diversity in music arose. I have known churches to crumble and leaders to falter due to the music program. Some insisted on Southern gospel, others contemporary, and others Christian rock. The question was posed: What type of music will our church favor?

I personally desired a modern genre, however I questioned if it was in that church's DNA. Understand that music is often a latch point where newcomers connect with formal worship and recognize that each church

---

150 Stephen A. Macchia, *Becoming a Healthy Church* (Grand Rapids, Mich.: BakerBooks, 1999), 47.

has its own flavor. A church is usually bent in the way it desires to go. If it is not progressive or open to certain new styles, one cannot coerce its members to go where they are not intended to go. I emphasized that whatever music is presented should be done to the best of our abilities, striving to always go to the next level. My response to the question of what type of music our church would favor made with mixed feelings and a bit of humor, was, "Our music will be whatever is the flavor of the day is. That's what it will be." I then noted that we would not know who would show up to play each day due the plague of commitment deficiencies meaning we have a dearth of musicians who would not commit to every service.

The discussion on diversity continued, and as a solution the group was simply asked, what will love cause us to do? The example of love that Jesus gave to us will overcome our differences and mold us into His unifying body due to our love for Christ and one for another. The diversity that necessitates unity affirms that the church has worked through its barriers culturally and relationally, developing love, acceptance, and forgiveness within its community.

How the church reacts to God's assignment determines the destiny of many souls. "The Church will transform the world to the degree that its people practice radical discipleship. To be world-changers, believers must first know they have passed from death to life. Then, they must be dissatisfied enough with a given state of affairs to bring about change."[151] The present reality of leadership is serving as examples endeavoring to build a community of faith under the rule of the King that is transmitted by the Holy Spirit delivering real radical love.

Evangelism

Leading an example of evangelism is imperative to the church, not for propagation of the gospel only but in obedience to the great commission as

---

151 John V. York, *Missions in the Age of the Spirit* (Springfield, Mo.: Logion Press, 2001), 176.

our Lord commanded so that none should perish. Believing everyone has the right to a presentation of the gospel on their level of understanding is a key value that will drive the church to make strategic decisions to focus on ministry with a priority of reaching the lost. Every believer has unique gifts to be developed and used to strengthen the church. Each one has a purpose in advancing the global goal of the body of Christ.

Jesus did not establish the church to be an end in itself. However, it was to carry on His ministry to the world. He charged believers to be His witnesses. When proclaimed properly the good news always carries with it the offer and power of salvation, which is the opportunity to receive forgiveness for sins and begin a relationship with God. "Evangelism is communicating the Gospel in an understandable manner and motivating a person to respond to Christ and become a responsible member of his church."[152] The important message of communicating the message of Christ is placed on the person of Christ and the uniqueness of His resurrection.

According to Romans 1:16, the preaching of the gospel is the power of God for salvation. William Martin says, "Witness and evangelism are a primary part of our mission as the church. And they involve what we say, how we act, what we are like on the inside, and how we are perceived by those to whom we witness."[153]

Evangelization is relational in respect to one's relationship to the Lord and those he or she is striving to reach. This can be facilitated as everyone integrates good deeds and good news into the life of a community, lifting Christ for all to see. God uses human instrumentality with hearts that are pliable and ready for service. Every Christian should be an evangel heralding the good news that Jesus saves.

Jesus emphasized evangelism with His last words to the followers. He commanded them in Matthew 28:19, "Therefore go and make disciples

---

152 Towns, 130.
153 Martin, 60.

of all nations." Jesus implies their purpose and calling is to evangelize. His charge to His followers was for them to be effectual witnesses in Jerusalem, Judea, Samaria, and the uttermost parts of the Earth. However, they were not to begin this staggering task until they had been equipped with the power of the Spirit (Acts 1:8).

The disciples were not sent on this venture of their own accord or on their own authority. Jesus commissioned them by saying, "All authority in heaven and on earth has been given to me" (Matthew 28:18). God's people are promised Christ's authority and power to proclaim the gospel throughout the world. The most powerful tool in the church's toolbox of ministry is not promotions, programs, or platforms. It is, however, the Spirit's empowerment to effectively witness.

The extent of this commission is all-inclusive with Jerusalem as the immediate vicinity to evangelize, then the Judean Jews on out. "Perhaps the most distasteful part of the commission for the disciples was the third part—'in Samaria.' This took them to the people whom they found most difficult to love, and who would probably be least receptive to their message because of being brought by Jews."[154] A worldview of evangelism is clearly depicted as barring any geographical restrictions as Jesus commanded the disciples to bear witness "to the ends of the earth" Acts 1:8. Realize that no one is beyond His love or reach.

Humanity is affected by a message that transcends race, creed, color, and class. "The practical challenge before churches today is to find creative ways to incarnate the gospel in their communities. Functioning in apostolic ministry is not the responsibility of only a few individuals. Rather, each congregation has a divine calling to participate with God in his mission to redeem the world. This is our primary task."[155]

---

154 Erickson, 1062.
155 Jay P. Taylor and Randy C. Walls. 2005. "Models of Apostolic Ministry: A Practical Theology Approach." *He Gave Apostles Apostolic Ministry in the 21ˢᵗ Century*, ed. Edgar R. Lee, 141. (Springfield, Mo.: Assemblies of God Theological Seminary.)

The desire to see the lost, least, and last of our world comes to know Christ experiencing His great love fuels our motivation. One's value and commitment drives the engine of evangelism to enlist effective outreach programs to saturate our world with the gospel. The goal is to use all available means in reaching people at all available times, enabling all to be a part of God's kingdom. God approaches the hearts of his people to impress His call to participate in His divine charge.

Overcoming the apathy of a sub cultural mindset is still a work in progress. The mission of Christ is to save that which is lost, and the church continues to adapt, finding ways to reach people with the gospel wherever they may be found. A nutshell strategy for church outreach and growth in the mission of God can be adopted with prayerful considerations from the heart of every Christian. First, decide to pray instead of panic. The task is not as overwhelming as it seems because one is led by Christ. Second, decide to be a missionary and not a mission field. Don't wait to be the witness you are meant to be. Third, decide to cast personal vision and define the mission God has for each person and what it means to each individual. Allow the Holy Spirit to come along your side for guidance and clarity in discerning God's will.

Fourth, decide to multiply instead of manage. God has designed His people to go give witness of His grace and add to the faith. He will manage the affairs of the kingdom. Fifth, decide to partner with a mentor. Seek out those who will invest in your spiritual well-being. Sixth, evangelize by deciding on a plan of action which is not an extracurricular activity but which is central to our purpose of existence. Strive to reach the un-churched, go for the MIAs (missing in attendance), and take love to our communities. Seventh, decide that fellowship builds relationships, and take it outside the church and win some to Christ. Eighth, decide that the Lord will build His church and the gates of hell will not prevail against it. God is for you.

Evangelism continues to infuse new growth into the kingdom. The church is heading in the right direction when a response to a water baptismal announcement is preceded by a new converts inquiry. This person possessed an intimidating appearance with tattoos from his face to his toes and jet-black hair hanging down to his elbows. Apparently fresh from the world, he came from a completely different context than most of the people in the church.

Standing up in the crowd with grave sincerity, he asked, "Next Sunday at the baptism do we go in naked as in some cultures, or what?" This had to be the best ending to one of the best services in my life, as it brought the world that we're to reach back into the church's view. This incident serves as a vivid reminder that our real business of reaching souls for Christ is in executing real evangelism with real compassion for real needs in a real world.

Compassion

Leading an example of Christ's compassion to all men is a model made effective by the power of the Holy Spirit in the believer's life. This lived-out paradigm enables one to partner with the Lord in engaging opportunities for Christian service, which are privileges and responsibilities of the household of faith. God's people exemplify Christ's compassion to His church by word and deed through servant leadership. Experiencing the love of God initiates a great love for one's neighbor who is made in the image of God. This influences us to minister compassionately to the hungry, sick, the lesser and down-trodden of society.

Crossing the Atlantic on board the ship *Arbella*, John Winthrop the first governor of the Massachusetts Bay Colony, delivered a sermon to the colonists on a model of Christian charity. Insights from his counsel encouraged the early colonists on how to display their love. Winthrop stated:

"We must entertain each other in brotherly affection. We must be willing to abridge ourselves of our superfluities, for the supply of others' necessities. We must uphold a familiar commerce together in all meekness, gentleness, patience, and liberality. We must delight in each other; make others' conditions our own; rejoice together, mourn together, labor and suffer together, always having before our eyes our commission and community in the work, as members of the same body."[156]

Encountering the example of Christ's compassion will characterize a life by selfless sharing wherever or however it is needed, which is the nature of radical discipleship. It is necessary for the church to provide for some people who lack initiative and moral force in which they cannot or will not do anything for themselves. Some troubles are due primarily to environments of exploitation and dehumanization or disaster. Regardless of the ills they must be assisted by charitable believers until they acquire means capable to meeting their own issues. Jesus said in Matthew 26:11 "The poor you will always have with you." God help us if we do not risk loving the unfortunate in our world.

"Thomas Aquinas claimed, 'If the primary aim of a captain were to preserve his ship, he would keep it in port forever.' The same goes for the church. If our goal is to preserve it, we will defensively protect it. If our goal is to reach out, to go somewhere, and to do something—we will willingly risk it."[157] There is a sense in which the church has refused to take the risk to go beyond its four walls. A spirit of holding the fort for us few and no more seems to prevail at times. The compassion of Christ compels us to go beyond the status quo. I've often thought that if you have nothing to risk, then what you have must not be worth much, yet love will risk it all.

---

156 William C. Placher, *Readings in the History of Christian Theology. Vol. 2.* (Louisville, Ky.: Westminster Press, 1988), 108–109.
157 Leith Anderson, *A Church for the 21ˢᵗ Century* (Minneapolis, Minn.: Bethany House Publishers, 1992), 185.

People of God must not withhold the love that was freely received as given by the Lord. Believers are encouraged to invest their lives for the good of others including time, talents, and resources allowing compassion to be manifest. Holy Scriptures declare in Proverbs 19:17 "He who is kind to the poor lends to the Lord, and he will reward him for what he has done." This goes beyond pity to offering a helping hand and meeting needs.

The Lord not only expresses concern for the needy, but expects His followers to recognize an obligation to care for the underprivileged which is the right ethical agenda to follow. In Mark 10:21 Jesus assured the rich young man treasures in heaven if he would sell everything he had and give to the poor. Benevolent giving is as lending to the Lord, an investment God will reward.

Many have become consumer-driven and have left the work of a charitable society due to a lack of self-missional purpose. There are those who are afraid of losing their power or personal glory within their communities. Some are focused on themselves rather than new ideas, ways, or outsiders and are fortifying a club of self-inclusion to hold on to their small empire. Instead, the church should practice repentance and determine to become a blessing to others and begin to exist for those who need to be reached in their community and world. Initiating a broader worldview will allow the church's example to be more open to the various cultures migrating into their communities.

For example, a rural congregation I had shepherd jumped several hurdles within five years. They received converted occult practitioners and drug dealers into the kingdom of God as well as a radically younger culture dressed with piercings, tattoos, and diversities of musical tastes. It was great to see a huge man with tats, a skinned head, body piercing and dressed cut-off sweats being surrounded by cultured small framed ladies in their Sunday frocks as they extended warm hugs of acceptance inquiring after his well-being.

A socioeconomic disparity existed yet no one seemed to care as they began to share a commonality in Christ. The primary purpose shifted from survival and maintenance mode that included a self-centered, self-serving mindset to an awareness of compassion and nurturing these recent converts. People rallied together with renewed evangelistic enthusiasm to reach their world. We must be open to loving people regardless of race, creed, background, class, economics, or other lifestyles. Know that Jesus will save and make the vilest of sinners His own.

> We have thought that keeping ourselves going is a good enough reason to continue. How different from Jesus, who came to seek and to save those who were lost (Luke 19:10). The church is really a means to an end rather than an end itself. God is the one who is most important. Obeying Jesus Christ is what really matters.[158]

It is important that shepherds have contact with their parishioners in order to connect and display who they are by example. Cultivating personal relationships that converse with and express genuine concern for the flock enables a rapport that unites a group to become strong inwardly yet externally focused. The need to stay in touch with the unsaved is imperative. Never forget how to relate in the world beyond the church walls.

It is right to lead by personal example. For instance, go the extra mile with others, and when a special financial need arises, strive to drop the first check in the collection plate or be the first volunteer for service. Refuse the need to be timid and release an assertive spirit not for self-exploitation but due to the demands of others' needs. Don't expect others to do something that you would not do. Let them clearly know you are more than willing to roll up your sleeves with them to do what it takes in reaching the common goal. People need assurance their leaders are in touch with the grassroots and can relate to the worldviews of the people they serve.

---

158 Anderson, 186.

Learn to lead within the circle of influence that promotes harmony and love for one another. Value others' strengths and giftedness, empowering them to be used for the edifying of the church's body with a kaleidoscope of talents and resources. While attending a presbyter's credentialing session, for example, the superintendent addressed the issue of culture. He exhorted the crowd with a profoundly moving message on the importance of reaching the boomers, builders, and busters in Arkansas. Afterward, the assistant superintendent said he would like to add another target group for us to reach. To the list of boomers, builders, and busters he added bubbas. Knowing your culture enables the church's understanding of those we are sent to reach. When we labor together for Christ, a magnificent representation of His presence is visibly on display so all may see and experience Him.

People in a church without an example of Christ's compassionate purpose usually see their participation as one activity alongside many activities in their lives, leading to the possibility of the church going nowhere. However, a church striving to live out His example focuses all of its activities around its involvement in God's mission in the world. The church trains and leads people in discipleship, witness, and worship and practices mutual support before the watching world by means of reaching, teaching, and sending forth. This church understands the prime example and commission of John 20:21. Just as God sent Jesus, now Jesus sends the church.

Yesterday's successes and failures are learned lessons, yet when change is needed, we cannot get stuck on the good old days. God has set us up for change in Proverbs 3:5–6. He requires us to trust in Him and to lean not on our own understanding but in all our ways acknowledge Him and He will make our paths straight. If God did not want us to change, why would we need to trust in Him? We could live in our comfortable existence and be content with what and who we are. However, no change means no faith required, and big changes often demand big faith. It takes a lot of love to undergo transitions that are beyond one's normal existence.

Every church like its community has a definite culture and culture does not always stay the same. Culture as defined by Gailyn Van Rheenen is the integrated system of learned patterns of ideas, values, behavior, products, and institutions characteristic of a society. We do not necessarily choose to join the existing culture, but we need to understand it.

> The moment we become like the people in a decaying church we lose our ability to help them rise to a new level. There are aspects of a culture that may be adopted without hindering one's ability to lead. Other ingrown traits, habits, and patterns are directly responsible for the downward trend and must be re-engineered. We begin by understanding culture before determining how or whether to go with it or change it. The wise pastor disciplines himself with a non-judgmental attitude. Listen, smile and commit yourself to nothing is good advice."[159]

For example, normally the status quo prevails in a rural setting. The bank, large amounts of land, local businesses, etc. are owned and operated by the same people. When you speak to them, they often refer to the good old days and say, "Yeah, things don't change much around here." The truth is, they don't. As a church driven by passionate leaders, we cannot afford to become the fortresses of the status quo.

Throughout America in huge metro cities to small townships few people in the church consider change a normal part of our lives and leaders strive to use their influence when change is needed.

> Yesterday McDonald's sold only hamburgers and fish; today you can eat breakfast there! In their vocations our people have been taught to think, how can we improve, expand our markets, do a better job? Yet, they have not been taught to think in these terms about the

---

159 Gene Wood, *Leading Turnaround Churches* (St. Charles, Ill.: ChurchSmart Resources, 2001), 138.

church. When they relate to the church and its ministries they shift from the city value of change to the rural value of maintaining the status quo. We church people embrace two value systems: one we apply to our work, our business, our "real" world and the other value system we apply to our church."[160]

Church leaders and congregations who are ineffective in their example of living a life unto Christ often seek only to maintain or hold on to the way things are. We are challenged to release old cultural norms and excess baggage in order to discover effective means to engage a real God who gives real hope to real people in a real world.

While fear, hatred, and violence grips the world, God's vision of "new creation" through reconciliation in Christ is desperately needed today. If Christians are to become part of today's solution socially and culturally, their doing so will require more than church as usual. We're learning not to be as inwardly focused but on the reign of God becoming a living sign and foretaste of God's new creation.

True Christianity is a force for righteousness and social improvement. Christians ought to direct their concerns to everything a person needs in a comprehensive approach by means of compassion through social activism.

A practical concern for health, diet, sanitation, agricultural improvement, land tenure, home and family, housing, education, literature, cottage industries, cooperatives, worship, evangelism, Christian stewardship and preaching are all inseparable parts of the Christian evangel. But these things must be conceived as indivisible elements of the gospel and must be *integrated* in the program of the church.[161]

---

160 Frank B. Tillapaugh, *Unleashing the Church* (Ventura, Calif.: Regal Books, 1982), 32.
161 Melvin L. Hodges, *A Theology of the Church and its Mission* (Springfield, Mo.: Gospel Publishing House, 1977), 99.

Jesus expressed concern and care regarding social problems. He encouraged those who wanted to follow Him to be concerned about the poor and help those less fortunate with financial aid (Matthew 19:21). "God's world as God's creation design is represented in every community/environment, and any changes taking place within this social and cultural context needs to be a matter of interest to a congregation. Spirit-led congregations have a dynamic relationship with the communities they seek to serve."[162] It is important that the church exerts compassion ministries to believers and non-believers alike. An act of compassion can be as simple as giving a cup of water to one who is thirsty.

The impact the church can make on society is accepting responsibility to perform acts of Christian love. Jesus expects His church to become involved with the needy and suffering. The parable of the Good Samaritan is clear evidence that Christ taught His disciples to have compassion for all people and what it means to love one's neighbor as oneself (Luke 10:25–37). "The new life and grace that Christ gives to those who accept Him will produce love, mercy, and compassion for those who are distressed and afflicted. It is the believer's responsibility to act upon the Holy Spirit's love within him and not to harden his heart."[163]

James defines true religion in the social context "to look after orphans and widows in their distress and to keep oneself from being polluted by the world" (James 1:27).

For General William Booth, founder of the Salvation Army, a church that is not passionately involved in ministering to the material needs of people falls drastically short of its commission to bring the gospel to all peoples. Yet he did not confuse faith in the gospel with love for our neighbor. The demonstration of Christian love prepares the way for commitment to the truth of the gospel as well as follows this commitment. His motto was "soup, soap and salvation," but he was

---

162 Van Gelder, *The Ministry of the Missional Church*, 143.
163 *The Full Life Study Bible, King James Version* (Zondervan Publishing, 1998), 1547.

adamant that our mission remains unfulfilled if we are concerned only with the first two and not with the last.[164]

The church is encouraged to speak out against atrocities, evil, and corruption. The Old Testament prophets were known to address issues of social corruption, and much like John the Baptist condemning Herod's sinfulness though doing so cost his life, they stood up against evil.

The church cannot hide its head in the sand whenever it sees hurt, wrongdoing, or unfulfilled needs. "In some cases, the church will work simply to alleviate the hurt, that is, to treat the consequences of the problem. In others, it will act to change the circumstances that have produced the problem. There will be times when the church acting collectively will be able to accomplish more than will Christians acting individually; in other situations the reverse will be true."[165]

The church reveals its true character and compassion as it emulates two attributes found in Christ, which are willingness to serve and adaptability. Jesus initiated servant hood as an example for the church to follow. He said His coming was not to be served but to serve (Matthew 20:28). Paul recognizes this in Philippians 2:7 when he writes that Jesus "made himself nothing, taking the very nature of a servant, being made in human likeness." As a servant, Jesus was always submissive to the Father's will, a fact which emphasizing the true nature of a servant.

"The church must display a similar willingness to serve. It has been placed in the world to serve its Lord and the world, not to be exalted and have its own needs and desires satisfied."[166] When the church serves willingly submitting itself to the Father's will, there is an abundance of pleasure and joy even though doing so may cost a grave price. The greater

---

164 Donald G. Bloesch, *The Church Sacraments, Worship, Ministry, Mission* (Downers Grove, Ill.: InterVarsity Press, 2002), 105.

165 Erickson, 1068.

166 Ibid., 1077.

price has been paid by the sacrifice Jesus provided. "You are not your own; you were bought at a price" (1 Corinthians 6:19-20).

The church continues to emulate the Lord who stepped out of His glory to undergo a great humiliation becoming a man and freely adapted to the confines of the world He created. God's people are resilient and adaptable as the palm trees of the desert. They have bent with the harsh winds of time and have remained versatile in adjusting methods and procedures within the changing world. Crisscrossing cultures, jumping religious barriers, and incurring persecution has enabled the church by the aid of the Holy Spirit to adapt in fulfilling the mission of God. The people of God do not alter their basic direction while adapting to the winds of change in effective ministry to society. The Lord's objectives are paramount to the church and are relevant to all humanity. The willingness to serve and adapt is motivated by a heart of compassion as is the heart of God.

CONCLUSION

PETER'S LETTER TO THE SHEPHERDS and people of God is as relevant now as it was when he wrote it. He challenged the believers who stood against the malicious persecutions directed against them. He reinforced the truth that believers are only strangers and pilgrims on Earth, passing through until heaven's shores are in view. He challenged believers to live a holy life with obedience and dedication, which was especially needed during this time of severe suffering.

The temptations were strong, compelling believers to return to the world they came from in order to save their lives and means. There are times when the strongest of Christians will want to throw in the towel, however that's when persistence, prayer, and faith kick into overdrive, delivering confidence that the Lord will see you through successfully.

The Christians were encouraged to live for the hope of salvation that is to come until Christ returns, indicating the social context of the family of God are here and now. If the people of God were to resist external pressures, then a high degree of group consciousness and unity was essential for their survival. To obtain their future reward (5:4) and eternal home, believers found themselves dependent upon one another safeguarding their fellowship in the Lord.

Their continuance came in the form of deference to one another. Instead of being disheartened due to their helplessness, displacement, and mistreatment by and from the world, the believers received encouragement, strength in their belief, and hope for the future. The empowered community of faith is today posed to minister to an offensive world without adopting a cynical and conquered state of mind.

Deterioration of a community and leadership often results from unwarranted pressures existing outside or within. Peter exhorts the elders how to lead under great duress by conducting their lives in a Godly manner. He encourages them in their suffering, identifying with their influential position to serve the church. Knowing these pastors were faced with temptations, Peter warned them to watch out for the corruption that would defile their ministries. Peter desired that pastors faithfully practice their service, giving to the task of shepherding the flock. At times when the heat is on and the minister finds himself in a fiery trial, he can always count on the one who called him to see him through.

The shepherd's role is to be motivated from an eager desire and not a begrudging spirit of necessity. Leaders should not be motivated by the dollar sign but for the love of ministry; not serve in search of power but because of how they can impact others; and not domineer but lead by examples. Shepherds are to safeguard the church and their own souls so they don't burn out, but burn brighter until the Lord of the harvest returns bringing a crown of glory to reward their service freely given unto Him.

There is a payoff at the end of a significant journey. Jesus Christ the Great Shepherd will come back "But the day of the Lord will come like a thief in the night ..." (2 Peter 3:10). The Scriptures state with assurance of Christ's arrival found in Revelation 22:7, "Behold, I am coming soon! Blessed is he who keeps the words of the prophecy in this book." With anticipation the laborers await His words "well done, good and faithful servant! You have been faithful with a few things; I will put you in charge of many things ..." (Matthew 25:21). At this juncture, God's people will reign with Him throughout all eternity. "After that, we who are still alive and are left will be caught up together with them in the clouds to meet the Lord in the air. And so we will be with the Lord forever" (1 Thessalonians 4:17).

Until the Lord's return, spiritual leadership is challenged to remain faithful to the primal task of shepherding the flock with moral and responsible applications. May one never cease to grow spiritually or intellectually. Maturation is not the end of the growth process only illumination to vaguely perceive how much is yet to be known. The exhortation found in 2 Peter 3:18 "But grow in grace and in the knowledge of our Lord and Savior Jesus Christ" does not end due to age or life experiences. Rather, growth in the Lord is a daily quest in one's relationship with God and/or world.

Execution of fair and balanced leadership is of grave importance. It is a good practice not to quickly pass a judgment on anyone until one can look into the eyes of their souls, try the spirit, and understand the intent of their hearts. The right disposition is a must as it determines how we perceive and handle situations and emotions. Attitudes oftentimes set forth the end results.

The primary goal of shepherds is to serve Christ in pursuit of reaching humanity with the good news of His love. God's pure love is a shepherd's guide for feeding the flock with all the aspects that accompany the charge. Love casts out fears when trials and temptations are set against us, allowing a place for courage to step up to fill a significant role. Whatever examples one leads with, may the legacy of a shepherd's journey reveal that love is not only its true intent, yet the outcome as well.

BIBLIOGRAPHY

Aalen, S. "Glory, Honour", ed. Colin Brown. *New International Dictionary of New Testament Theology*, vol. 2. Grand Rapids, Mich.: Zondervan, 1986.

Aker, Benny C. and Edgar R. Lee. "Naturally Supernatural: The Baptism of the Spirit," *Signs & Wonders in Ministry Today*. Eds. Benny C. Aker & Gary B. McGee. Springfield, Mo: Gospel Publishing House, 1996.

Anders, Max. *Holman New Testament Commentary*. Nashville, Tenn.: Broadman & Holman Publishers, 1999.

Anderson, Leith. *A Church for the 21st Century*. Minneapolis, Minn.: Bethany House Publishers, 1992.

Barna, George. *Leaders on Leadership*. Ventura, Calif.: Regal, 1997.

Berkouwer, William B. *Studies in Dogmatics The Church*. Grand Rapids, Mich.: Eerdmans, 1976.

Beyreuther, E. "Shepherd" *The New International Dictionary of New Testament Theology*, vol. 3. Grand Rapids, Mich.: Zondervan, 1971.

Block, Daniel I. The Burden of Leadership: *The Mosaic Paradigm of Kingship.* Bibliotheca Sacra Jul/Sep 2005.

Bloesch, Donald G. *The Church Sacraments, Worship, Ministry, Mission.* Downers Grove, Ill.: InterVarsity Press, 2002.

Boring, M. Eugene. *Abingdon New Testament Commentaries: I Peter.* Nashville, Tenn.: Abingdon Press, 1999.

Bridges, James K. *Pentecostal Gifts & Ministries in a Postmodern Era.* Springfield, Mo.: Gospel Publishing House, 2004.

Bruce, F. F., D.D., F.B.A. *The Gospel of John.* Grand Rapids, Mich.: Eerdmans, 1983.

Burge, Gary M. *John The NIV Application Commentary.* Grand Rapids, Mich.: Eerdmans, 2003.

Coenen, L. *New International Dictionary of New Testament Theology*, vol. 1. Ed. Colin Brown. Grand Rapids, Mich.: Zondervan, 1986.

Cotton, Roger D. "Walking in the Spirit in Spontaneity." *Paraclete 25/1.* Springfield, Mo.: Gospel Publishing House, 1991.

Davids, Peter H. *The First Epistle of Peter.* Grand Rapids, Mich.: Eerdmans, 1990.

Edersheim, Alfred. *The Life and Times of Jesus the Messiah.* Grand Rapids, Mich.: Eerdmans, 1980.

Elliott, John H. *Home for the Homeless*. Eugene, Ore.: Wipf and Stock Publishers, 2005.

Erickson, Millard J. *Christian Theology*, 2nd ed. Grand Rapids, Mich.: Baker Books, 1998.

Gärtner, B. *Shepherd*, ed. Colin Brown. *New International Dictionary of New Testament Theology*, vol. 3. Grand Rapids, Mich.: Zondervan, 1986.

Gee, Donald. *After Pentecost*. Springfield, Mo.: Gospel Publishing House, 1945.

Gibbs, Eddie. *Leadership Next: Changing Leaders in a Changing Culture*. Downers Grove, Ill.: InterVarsity, 2005.

Glasser, Arthur F. *Announcing the Kingdom*. Grand Rapids, Mich.: Baker Academic, 2007.

Goppelt, Leonhard. *A Commentary on 1 Peter*. Grand Rapids, Mich.: Eerdmans, 1993.

Harrup, J. Lowell. "The Ministry and Gifts of the Holy Spirit Today: Cooperating with the Spirit," *Enrichment 10*, no.1 (Winter 2005).

Harder, G. *Soul*, ed. Colin Brown. *New International Dictionary of New Testament Theology*, vol. 3. Grand Rapids, Mich.: Zondervan, 1986.

Hemer, C. J. *New International Dictionary of New Testament Theology, vol. 1*. Ed. Colin Brown. Grand Rapids, Mich.: Zondervan, 1986.

Hernando, James D. *Dictionary of Hermeneutics*. Springfield, Mo.: Gospel Publishing House, 2005.

Hodges, Melvin L. *A Theology of the Church and its Mission*. Springfield, Mo.: Gospel Publishing House, 1977.

Horton, Stanley M. *What the Bible Says about the Holy Spirit*. Springfield, Mo.: Gospel Publishing House, 2005.

Jeffrey, Grant R. *Heaven The Last Frontier*. Toronto, Ontario, Canada: Frontier Research Publications, 1990.

Jeremias, J. *Theological Dictionary of the New Testament*. Ed. G. Kittel, G. W. Bromiley & G. Friedrich (electronic ed.). Grand Rapids, Mich.: Eerdmans, 1976.

Jobes, Karen H. *I Peter*. Grand Rapids, Mich.: Baker Academic, 2005.

Keener, C. S. *The IVP Bible Background Commentary: New Testament*. Downers Grove, Ill.: Intervarsity Press, 1993.

Keener, Craig S. *Gift & Giver*. Grand Rapids, Mich.: Baker Academic, 2001.

Köstenberger, Andreas J. and Peter T. O'Brien. *Salvation to the Ends of the Earth*. Downers Grove, Ill.: InterVarsity Press, 2006.

Kraiss, Wayne. "The Pastor as Shepherd." *The Pentecostal Pastor a Mandate for the 21st Century*. Compiled and edited by Thomas E. Trask, Wayde I. Goodall, and Zenas J. Bicket, 203-212. Springfield, Mo.: Gospel Publishing House, 2006.

Kruse, Colin G. *The Gospel According to John*. Grand Rapids, Mich.: Eerdmans, 2003.

Lee, Edgar R. STD. "Systematic Theology II." Class notes for Unit 4 Ecclesiology at Assemblies of God Theological Seminary. Springfield, Mo.: 3 July, 2008.

Lewis, C.S. *Mere Christianity*. New York: MacMillan, 1952.

Lewis, Robert. *The Church of Irresistible Influence*. Grand Rapids, Mich.: Zondervan, 2001.

Lim, David. *Spiritual Gifts: A Fresh Look*. Springfield, Mo.: Gospel Publishing House, 2003.

Macchia, Stephen A. *Becoming a Healthy Church*. Grand Rapids, Mich.: BakerBooks, 1999.

Marshall, Howard I. *The IVP New International Commentary Series: I Peter*. Downers Grove, Ill.: InterVarsity Press, 1991.

Martin, William J. *The Church in Mission*. Springfield, Mo.: Gospel Publishing House, 1996.

Mattingly, Gerald L. *Shepherd*. Ed. P. J. Achtemeier, P. *Harper's Bible Dictionary,* 1st ed. San Francisco, Calif.: Harper & Row, 1985.

Maxwell, John C. *The 21 Irrefutable Laws of Leadership*. Nashville, Tenn.: Thomas Nelson, 1998.

McKnight, Scot. *I Peter. The NIV Application Commentary.* Grand Rapids, Mich.: Zondervan, 1996.

Menzies, Robert P. "Coming to Terms With an Evangelical Heritage—Part 2: Pentecostals and Evidential Tongues." *Paraclete 28/4.* Springfield, Mo.: Gospel Publishing House, 1994.

Menzies, William W. and Robert P. Menzies. *Spirit and Power.* Grand Rapids, Mich.: Zondervan, 2000.

Müller, D. *Will*, Ed. Colin Brown. *New International Dictionary of New Testament Theology*, vol. 3. Grand Rapids, Mich.: Zondervan, 1986.

Osborne, G. R. *Elder.* eds. J. B. Green, S. McKnight, and I. H. Marshall. *Dictionary of Jesus and the Gospels.* Downers Grove, Ill.: InterVarsity Press, 1992.

Palma, Anthony D. *Holy Spirit a Pentecostal Perspective.* Springfield, Mo.: Gospel Publishing House, 2001.

Placher, William C. *Readings in the History of Christian Theology, Vols. 1 & 2.* Louisville, Ky.: Westminster Press, 1988.

Ryken, L., J. Wilhoit, T. Longman, C. Duriez, D. Penney, and D. G. Reid. *Dictionary of Biblical Imagery* (electronic ed.). Downers Grove, Ill.: InterVarsity Press, 2000.

Siede, B. κερδοσ *(kerdos),* ed. Colin Brown. vol. 3 of *New International Dictionary of New Testament Theology*, vol. 3. Grand Rapids, Mich.: Zondervan, 1986.

Stibbs, Alan M. *The First Epistle General of Peter*. Grand Rapids, Mich.: Eerdman's, 1978.

Strong, James. *The Exhaustive Concordance of the Bible* (electronic ed.). Ontario: Woodside Bible Fellowship, 1996.

Swindoll, Chuck. *Improving Your Serve*. Waco, Tex.: Word, 1981.

Tan, Paul Lee. *Encyclopedia of 7,700 Illustrations*. Rockville, Md.: Assurance Publishers, 1984.

Tasker, R. V. G., M.A., B.D. *The Gospel According to St. John*. Grand Rapids, Mich.: Eerdman's, 1978.

Taylor, Jay P. and Randy C. Walls. "Models of Apostolic Ministry: A Practical Theology Approach." *He Gave Apostles Apostolic Ministry in the 21ˢᵗ Century*. Ed. Edgar R. Lee, Springfield, Mo.: Assemblies of God Theological Seminary, 2005.

Thurén, Lauri. *Argument and Theology in I Peter: The Origins of Christian Paraenesis*, series 114. Sheffield, England.: Sheffield Academic Press, 1995.

Tillapaugh, Frank. *Unleashing the Church*. Ventura, Calif.: Regal Books, 1982.

Towns, Elmer L. and Ed Stetzer. *Perimeters of Light Biblical Boundaries for the Emerging Church*. Chicago: Moody Publishers, 2004.

Van Gelder, Craig. *The Essence of the Church*. Grand Rapids, Mich.: BakerBooks, 2007.

Van Gelder, Craig. *The Ministry of the Missional Church*. Grand Rapids, Mich. BakerBooks, 2007.

Vincent, M. R. *Word Studies in the New Testament*. Bellingham, Wash.: Logos Research Systems, 2002.

Wood, D. R. W. *New Bible Dictionary*. Downers Grove, Ill.: InterVarsity Press, 1996.

Wood, Gene. *Leading Turnaround Churches*. St. Charles, Ill.: ChurchSmart Resources, 2001.

York, John V. *Missions in the Age of the Spirit*. Springfield, Mo.: Logion Press, 2001.